WHISTLING WHILE THEY WORK

Roberts | Brown | Olsen

WHISTLING WHILE THEY WORK

A good-practice guide for managing internal reporting of wrongdoing in public sector organisations

Peter Roberts *Charles Sturt University*

A. J. Brown *Griffith University*

Jane Olsen *NSW Ombudsman's Office*

ANU
THE AUSTRALIAN NATIONAL UNIVERSITY

E PRESS

ANU
E PRESS

Published by ANU E Press

The Australian National University
Canberra ACT 0200, Australia

Email: anuepress@anu.edu.au

This title is also available online at: http://epress.anu.edu.au

National Library of Australia Cataloguing-in-Publication entry

Author:	Roberts, Peter.
Title:	Whistling while they work : a good-practice guide for managing internal reporting of wrongdoing in public sector organisations / Peter Roberts, A. J. Brown, Jane Olsen.
ISBN	9781921862304 (pbk.) 9781921862311 (eBook)
Notes:	Includes bibliographical references.
Subjects:	Whistle blowing. Disclosure of information. Public administration.
Other Authors/Contributors:	Olsen, Jane. Brown, A. J. (Alexander Jonathan)
Dewey Number:	352.439

Cover design and layout by luxgraphicus (http://www.luxgraphicus.com)

Contents

ABOUT THE AUTHORS

Peter Roberts is Senior Lecturer, Australian Graduate School of Policing, Charles Sturt University, and a former senior executive with the Commonwealth Attorney-General's Department and the National Crime Authority. Email: <peroberts@csu.edu.au>

A. J. Brown is John Kearney Professor of Public Law, Griffith Law School, Griffith University, and project leader of the Whistling While They Work project. He is also a former Senior Investigation Officer with the Commonwealth Ombudsman. Email: <A.J.Brown@griffith.edu.au>

Jane Olsen is a Project Officer, Public Interest Disclosures Unit, NSW Ombudsman. She is a former Research Officer, Research and Prevention Unit, Crime and Misconduct Commission (Queensland), and Senior Research Assistant, Socio-Legal Research Centre, Griffith University. Email: <jolsen@ombo.nsw.gov.au>

ACKNOWLEDGEMENTS

This guide is based on research conducted in the national project 'Whistling While They Work: Enhancing the Theory and Practice of Internal Witness Management in the Australian Public Sector' (see: <http://www.griffith.edu.au/whistleblowing>). This research was made possible by the Australian Research Council (Linkage Project 0560303) and the project's partner organisations:

Commonwealth	Commonwealth Ombudsman
	Australian Public Service Commission
New South Wales	Independent Commission Against Corruption
	NSW Ombudsman
Queensland	Crime and Misconduct Commission
	Queensland Ombudsman
	Office of the Public Service Commissioner
Western Australia	Corruption and Crime Commission
	Ombudsman Western Australia
	Office of the Public Sector Standards Commissioner
Victoria	Ombudsman Victoria
Northern Territory	Commissioner for Public Employment
Australian Capital Territory	Chief Minister's Department
Non-government partner	Transparency International Australia

The authors thank all project partners and colleagues for their support and contributions to these results. Special thanks to the case-study organisations and their enthusiastic representatives who provided invaluable information on managing whistleblowing in practice. Additional thanks to Professor David Lewis, Middlesex University, United Kingdom; Professor Terry Dworkin, Seattle and Indiana Universities, United States of America; and Peter Bennett, National Whistleblowing Information Centre (Australia) for many helpful comments on the draft of this guide.

The findings and views expressed are those of the authors and do not necessarily represent the views of the Australian Research Council or the partner organisations in the project.

INTRODUCTION

Whistleblowing is the 'disclosure by organisation members (former or current) of illegal, immoral or illegitimate practices under the control of their employers, to persons or organisations that may be able to effect action' (Miceli and Near 1984).

This guide sets out results from four years of research into how public sector organisations can better fulfil their missions, maintain their integrity and value their employees by adopting a current best-practice approach to the management of whistleblowing.

Whistleblowing is the 'disclosure by organisation members (former or current) of illegal, immoral or illegitimate practices under the control of their employers, to persons or organisations that may be able to effect action' (Miceli and Near 1984). This guide focuses especially on

- the processes needed for public employees and employees of public contractors to be able to report concerns about wrongdoing in public agencies and programs
- managerial responsibilities for the support, protection and management of those who make disclosures about wrongdoing, as part of an integrated management approach.

The guide is designed to assist with the special systems needed for managing 'public interest' whistleblowing—where the suspected or alleged wrongdoing affects more than the personal or private interests of the person making the disclosure. As the guide explains, however, an integrated approach requires having good systems for managing *all* types of reported wrongdoing—including personal, employment and workplace grievances—not least because these might often be interrelated with 'public interest' matters.

There are four reasons why it is important for public sector managers to recognise, and properly manage, the role of whistleblowing in their organisation

- it is increasingly accepted that employee reporting is often the most effective and fastest way for senior management of organisations to become aware of problems in their organisation
- if organisations do *not* manage whistleblowing effectively, it is now well known that complaints are more likely to be taken outside the organisation, including into the public domain, leading to greater conflict, embarrassment and cost
- organisations that support employees in fulfilling their duty to report concerns are more likely to become known as good workplaces and employers of choice, while organisations who do not are more likely to become liable for failing to provide employees with a safe, healthy and professional working environment
- public sector agencies are increasingly subject to specific statutory obligations to manage whistleblowing to a high standard, as part of their jurisdiction's public integrity systems.

In Australia, requirements for improved internal disclosure procedures (IDPs), including better provision for employee protection and support, are set out in the *Public Interest Disclosure Acts* of all State and Territory jurisdictions. This includes new *Public Interest Disclosure Acts* passed in Queensland and New South Wales in September and October 2010, and new legislation promised at the Commonwealth level.

These developments have also led and been informed by parallel recognition of the importance of whistleblowing for the management of all organisations, including in the business and civil society sectors. In 2003, the *Australian Standard on Whistleblower Protection Programs for Entities* (AS 8004-2003) was published; and in 2004, whistleblower protection provisions were inserted in Part 9.4AAA of the *Corporations Act 2001* (Cwlth). Like public sector provisions, these are subject to review and are likely to be upgraded.

With these imperatives in mind, this guide sets out a framework that public sector agencies—large and small—can use to develop and implement improved IDPs for their own organisation.

DEVELOPMENT OF THE GUIDE

The guide was produced as part of an Australian Research Council-funded Linkage Project, 'Whistling While They Work: Enhancing the Theory and Practice of Internal Witness Management in Public Sector Organisations' (2005–09).

The project collected data from more than 300 Commonwealth, State and local agencies in Australia, including individual survey responses from more than 10,000 public employees, managers and case-handlers (persons involved in the investigation and management of reported wrongdoing). Many of the empirical data were reported in Whistleblowing in the Australian Public Sector (Brown 2008), published by the Australia and New Zealand School of Government and ANU E Press (<http://epress.anu.edu.au/whistleblowing_citation.html>).

In addition to the empirical data already reported, this guide presents new research based on the experience of 16 Commonwealth, State and local case-study agencies who participated in depth throughout the project. The features of these agencies and the research undertaken are set out in Appendix I. The additional research underpinning the guide includes

- further quantitative analysis of empirical data, including extensive comparative analyses of data from the 16 case-study agencies

- qualitative data obtained from 92 interviews of internal witnesses, managers, investigators and support staff from the case-study agencies, as well as the free text responses to the larger surveys

- results of a series of workshops attended by the representatives of the case-study agencies and partner organisations over a four-year period.

Earlier outputs based on this research, including a draft version of this guide released at the second Australian Public Sector Anti-Corruption Conference (Brisbane, July 2009), have already informed the development of official procedures and advice in a number of Australian governments (see, for example, Crime and Misconduct Commission et al. 2009; NSW Ombudsman 2009). Many valuable comments were received on the draft, as well as the additional research and analysis that inform this guide.

The result is a new framework based on the practical experience of a diverse range of organisations. The framework will help organisations understand and put in place the five elements of a best-practice whistleblowing program

A. organisational commitment to good management of whistleblowing

B. facilitating reporting

C. assessment and investigation of reports

D. internal witness support and protection

E. an integrated organisational approach.

This guide should be used to inform the way that organisations implement the statutory objectives of most public interest disclosure legislation

- to encourage public officials to report wrongdoing within or by their organisation, to those who can effect action
- to ensure effective action, including investigation, in response to those reports
- to ensure that employees who report wrongdoing are supported and protected from adverse consequences that can flow from having fulfilled their duty to report.

The guide is structured to provide public sector organisations with three things.

1. Program framework and checklist

Within the five fundamental elements of a whistleblowing program listed above, the guide breaks down into a number of sub-elements and a checklist of the key items that should be addressed by any organisation wishing to develop and implement a successful program.

The checklist is set out at the end of this Introduction. The guide then presents and discusses each sub-element along with the checklist items.

The framework and checklist evolved from comparison of the main institutional elements and strategies that made up different organisations' approaches to the management of whistleblowing. This commenced at a symposium held in Canberra in July 2005, by the project and the Australia and New Zealand School of Government.

A first-draft framework was developed based on 24 items used in the assessment of the comprehensiveness of written agency procedures (Roberts 2008:245). These included the 14 items suggested by the checklist in the *Australian Standard on Whistleblower Protection Programs for Entities* (AS 8004-2003).

The framework was then developed through discussion among case-study agencies and partner organisations at three case-study workshops, held in July 2007, July 2008 and September 2008. These workshops discussed data relevant to the performance of agencies' approaches, and shared experience of those approaches. The final framework and checklist reflect the collective experience of a large body of research and a diverse group of agencies.

2. Commentary and explanation

Under each element and sub-element, the guide summarises the key relevant issues and lessons from the research, including the experiences of agencies, and insights from the 92 interviews with whistleblowers, managers and case-handlers.

A key philosophy underpinning the guide is to maximise and properly manage whistleblowing by adopting a policy of 'if in doubt, report', to encourage the reporting of wrongdoing. In practice, this translates into policies that do not filter or set artificial administrative thresholds for receiving reports, but rather encourage staff to bring forward any issue that is concerning them. The research confirms that it is better for organisations to receive too much information about wrongdoing than too little, or too late.

A second key philosophy—and a direct corollary of an 'if in doubt, report' approach—is that organisations must accept their obligations to take reports seriously, respond appropriately and professionally (even if the outcome is no action), and support and protect persons who come forward with reports of wrongdoing.

This last area was revealed by the research to be the element with which most organisations continue to struggle (Brown and Olsen 2008a). In line with strengthened statutory requirements, the guide is aimed at helping organisations realise the potential for developing improved tools and strategies for ensuring the health, safety and wellbeing of officials who fulfil their public duty to report wrongdoing.

3. Practical action

Each section of the guide lists practical actions that agencies can take to address the issues raised. Practical action includes developing, promulgating and implementing better procedures, which the research showed were directly related to employees having higher confidence in the likely response of management to disclosures, as well as to better substantive outcomes (Roberts 2008:255–8).

Some sections of the guide therefore also provide diagrams, flow charts and sample language for written procedures, drawing on approaches taken by the agencies who participated in the research and, in particular, the NSW Ombudsman's Office and the Crime and Misconduct Commission. These sample procedures are not intended to be adopted word-for-word by organisations, but used as a starting point for the drafting or redrafting of policies and procedures, in line with organisations' different legislative requirements, operating environments and needs.

The authors thank the case-study organisations for their pivotal role in the production of this guide, and trust it will help lead to better outcomes for the bulk of organisations committed to public accountability, integrity and organisational justice.

THE CHECKLIST:

REQUIRED ELEMENTS FOR A WHISTLEBLOWING PROGRAM

A. Organisational Commitment

A1. Management commitment

- Clear statements by senior management of the organisation's support for the reporting of wrongdoing through appropriate channels ('if in doubt, report'), including commitments to
  - take credible and appropriate action upon receipt of a whistleblowing report
  - remedy any confirmed wrongdoing
  - support whistleblowers.
- Commitment to the principles of whistleblowing among first and second-level managers, including
  - understanding of the benefits and importance of whistleblowing mechanisms

- knowledge of and confidence in whistleblowing policies.
- Broad staff confidence in management responsiveness to whistleblowing.

A2. Whistleblowing policy

- Easy to comprehend whistleblowing policy, including guidance on procedures, relationship with other procedures and legal obligations.
- Broad staff awareness of the whistleblowing program and policy, including their responsibility to report possible wrongdoing.

A3. Resources

- Staffing and financial resources dedicated to implementation and maintenance of the program, commensurate with organisational size and needs.
- Specialised training for key personnel, including whistleblowing management issues as part of general induction and management training.

A4. Evaluation and engagement

- Regular evaluation and continual improvement in the program.
- Positive engagement on whistleblowing issues with external integrity agencies, staff associations and client groups.

B. Facilitating Reporting

B1. Who may report wrongdoing?

- Clear and comprehensive approach to including all key categories of organisation members (for example, employees, contractors, employees of contractors, volunteers) in the program.

B2. What should be reported?

- Clear procedures and advice to staff on
  - the types of wrongdoing that should be reported
  - appropriate reporting points for all different types of wrongdoing (including grievances as opposed to public interest disclosures)
  - the level of information required/desired in a report.
- Clear advice that staff
  - are not protected from the consequences of their own wrongdoing by reporting it, nor for deliberately providing false or misleading information
  - may nevertheless seek and be granted immunity from consequences from their own less serious wrongdoing, when reporting other more serious wrongdoing.

B3. Multiple reporting pathways

- Clear advice on *to whom* and *how* whistleblowing reports should be made, including
  - *internal* reporting paths
  - *alternatives* to direct line reporting (that is, guidance on when staff should consider reporting outside the normal management chain)

- *external* reporting paths, including external (contracted) hotlines and relevant regulatory or integrity agencies, and when these should be approached in the first instance.
- Clear advice regarding disclosures to the media.

B4.Anonymity
- Clear advice that anonymous reports will be acted upon wherever possible, and about how anonymous reports/approaches may be made.

C. Assessment and Investigation of Reports

C1.Identification and tracking of reports
- A coordinated system for tracking all significant reports of wrongdoing (including grievances) at all levels of the organisation, including clear advice to supervisors on when, how and whom to notify about staff complaints and possible whistleblowing reports.
- Organisational procedure for mandatory reporting to regulatory or integrity agencies on whistleblowing reports, including early notification of significant or higher-risk reports.

C2.Assessment procedures
- Management procedures and skills for differentiating, as appropriate, between different types of wrongdoing (including grievances), and initiating appropriate action.
- A flexible approach to the types, level and formality of investigations to be conducted, including clear criteria for when no further action is required.
- Early and continuing assessment of the risks of reprisal, workplace conflict or other adverse outcomes involving whistleblowers or other witnesses.

C3.Confidentiality
- Commitment to the confidentiality of whistleblowing reports to the maximum extent possible, including
  - procedures for maintaining the confidentiality of whistleblowers, persons against whom allegations have been made, and other witnesses to the maximum extent possible
  - clear advice about possible limits of confidentiality
  - procedures for consulting and, wherever possible, gaining consent of whistleblowers prior to any action that could identify them, including to external agencies.
- Procedures for determining when confidentiality cannot be ensured, and active strategies for supporting employees and managing workplaces where confidentiality is not possible or cannot be maintained.

C4.Equity and natural justice
- Clear procedures for the protection of the rights of persons against whom allegations have been made, including appropriate sanctions against

- false or vexatious allegations

- unreasonable breaches of confidentiality.

- Clear advice to managers about to whom, when and by whom information about allegations of wrongdoing need be given, for reasons such as natural justice.

D. Internal Witness Support and Protection

D1.Whistleblower/internal witness support

- A proactive support strategy for organisation members who report wrongdoing (that is, management initiated and not simply complaint/ concern driven), including

  - designation of one or more officers with responsibility for establishing and coordinating a support strategy appropriate to each whistleblowing case

  - support arrangements tailored to identified risks of reprisal, workplace conflict or other adverse outcomes.

- Risk assessment and support decision making that directly involve

  - the whistleblower(s) or other witnesses involved

  - the identification and involvement of agreed support person(s) (for example, 'confidants', 'mentors', 'interview friends' or similar), with agreed roles.

D2.Information and advice

- Timely provision of information, advice and feedback to reporters and witnesses about

  - the actions being taken in response to disclosure

  - reasons for actions (including no action)

  - how to manage their role in the investigation process, including whom to approach regarding issues or concerns regarding reprisals

  - ultimate outcomes, benefits to the organisation, and remedial change.

- Provision of information, advice and access to

  - appropriate professional support services (for example, stress management, counselling, legal, independent career counselling)

  - external regulatory or integrity agencies that may be accessed for support.

D3.Preventing and remedying detrimental action

- Clear commitment that the organisation will not undertake disciplinary or adverse actions, or tolerate reprisals by anyone in the organisation including managers, as a result of disclosures.

- Mechanisms for ensuring that

  - the welfare of organisation members who report wrongdoing is monitored from the point of first report

  - positive workplace decisions are taken for preventing, containing and addressing risks of conflict and reprisal

  - supervisors or alternative managers are directly engaged in risk assessment, support decision making and workplace decisions, to the maximum extent possible.

- Clear authority for support personnel to involve higher authorities (for example, CEO, audit committee and external agencies) in whistleblower management decisions.
- Specialist expertise for investigating alleged detrimental actions or failures in support, with automatic notification of such allegations to relevant external agencies.
- Flexible mechanisms for compensation or restitution in the event of any failure to provide adequate support, or prevent or contain adverse outcomes.

D4. Exit and follow-up strategy

- Exit strategies for concluding organised support to whistleblowers.
- Follow-up monitoring of whistleblower welfare, as part of regular evaluation of program and to identify ongoing, unreported support needs.

E. An Integrated Organisational Approach

E1. Clear organisational model for support

- Clear information for managers and staff about the support strategies employed by the organisation (that is, 'standing', 'devolved', 'case-by-case').
- Clear understanding of whistleblowing-related roles and responsibilities of key players, internal and external to the organisation.
- Operational separation of investigation and support functions.
- Clear and direct lines of reporting from support personnel to audit/integrity committee and/or CEO, and external agencies.

E2. Shared responsibility for whistleblower support

- Clear lines of communication to ensure managers retain responsibility for their workplace and staff to the maximum extent possible.
- Clear lines of communication with external agencies regarding the incidence, nature and status of active cases.

E3. Embedded policies and procedures

- Integrated and coordinated procedures (not 'layered' or 'alternative').
- Integrated complaint/incident recording and management systems.
- Whistleblower support integrated into human resources, career development and workplace health and safety (WH&S) policies.

A.

ORGANISATIONAL COMMITMENT

Organisational commitment refers to the acceptance that an organisation has an obligation to promote reporting of wrongdoing and to protect employees who come forward with reports.

Legislative provisions and black-letter procedures can go only so far in creating an effective whistleblower reporting and protection regime. The research has shown that an essential ingredient in any whistleblowing program is the commitment from each organisation to encourage reporting, act on the reports where appropriate and to protect reporters from any adverse consequences.

Organisational commitment also has a specific meaning in organisational psychology. In the range of attitudes studied in organisational behaviour, organisational commitment sits beside job satisfaction and job involvement as 'a state in which an employee identifies with a particular organisation and its goals, and wishes to maintain membership in the organisation' (Robbins et al. 2008:80).

Organisational commitment, in the context of whistleblowing, comprehends the degree to which the organisation as an entity deals with whistleblowing. Achieving strong commitment involves

- *policies and procedures* that signify the formal acceptance by the organisation of the principles of encouragement of reporting and protection of whistleblowers

- *leadership*—energy and commitment exhibited by senior management towards ensuring that there is no mismatch between the commitment outlined in the procedures and actual practice within the organisation, including allocation of financial and human resources

- *line managers* are usually the first point where reports are received, and they have the immediate responsibility for the wellbeing of employees; thus line managers warrant being looked at separately

- *reporters* need to trust that the procedures are adequate and that the commitment from those above them is such that their reports will be acted upon and they will be protected. A particular element of organisational commitment for reporters is their trust in management.

There is a strong link between the ethical climate of an organisation (part of the organisational culture) and effective whistleblowing policies and procedures. Where there is a good ethical climate and leadership support for whistleblowing, the experience of the case-study agencies is that good results will follow (see Wortley et al. 2008:71, Table 3.12).

Underpinning the elements below, strong organisational commitment was indicated by

- a culture of integrity in the organisation, and commitment to whistleblowing and the protection of reporters as a key component of that culture, manifested in a code of conduct

- involvement in the whistleblowing procedures at all levels of management, since line managers are the most likely recipients of staff concerns and need to fully understand the organisation's attitudes, policies and procedures in relationship to whistleblowing.

In many organisations, senior executives clearly recognise arguments in support of whistleblowing that

- stress the value of compliance with government policies and legislation

- demonstrate efficiency, including the benefits to the organisation of identifying fraud or defective practices, and of investing in awareness raising, training and internal witness support as a means of reducing the number of whistleblowing cases that become difficult, complex, time-consuming and costly.

If, however, senior managers in an organisation do not act ethically themselves, the effort being put into whistleblowing policies and procedures can also be largely wasted. The phrase 'walk the talk' was used frequently in interviews and workshops. A disturbing criticism made about leadership in the area of whistleblowing was that many managers publicly supported the process but privately acted against it. Put another way, words and actions do not reconcile.

A number of factors can indicate the absence of an organisational commitment to whistleblowing, including

- a culture of secretiveness and cover-ups ('butt covering') when staff make disclosures

- a 'shoot the messenger' culture when unpleasant issues are raised

- disregarding a staff member's report as merely being that person's personal perception

- gossip as the major channel of communication about wrongdoing

- the use of derogatory language (even privately) in referring to staff members who make disclosures

- damage to the careers of staff members who make disclosures.

TRUST

Trust is an essential part of a successful whistleblowing policy, and a key indicator of organisational commitment. While trust can be looked at as an issue primarily for employees contemplating reporting wrongdoing, it is also an issue for line managers. If managers accept that the organisation is genuinely committed to the principles of wrongdoing then their belief will enhance the trust of employees at lower levels in the organisation.

The empirical research demonstrated the importance of trust in building effective whistleblowing programs.

1 High levels of trust in the organisation are associated with decisions to report wrongdoing—a very important finding, given that most reporting is internal to organisations (Wortley et al. 2008:60, Table 3.4).

2 At an individual level, trust in the recipient of the report is an important factor in the decision about reporting pathways, in particular the selection of internal reporting pathways over external reporting pathways (Donkin et al. 2008:103).

3 Building trust can be expected to maximise the amount of wrongdoing that is reported and encourage issues to be reported quickly rather than festering and developing into more serious problems (Donkin et al. 2008:106).

4 Where employees formed a view that they would be protected and supported by management if they reported wrongdoing, they were more likely to do so (Donkin et al. 2008:106).

5 Knowledge of legislation is associated with higher levels of trust, as are knowledge of agency whistleblowing procedures and the comprehensiveness of those procedures (Roberts 2008:243, Table 10.7).

Achieving trust is nevertheless not a simple issue. All reporters showed a decline in trust of their organisation, even those reporters who were not treated badly by the reporting experience (Donkin et al. 2008:102). Lower levels of trust in management were also found where the wrongdoing was aimed at the reporter (Wortley et al. 2008:69, Table 3.9).

While the interviews of managers and case-handlers confirmed the important part that trust played in a successful whistleblower protection policy, the 58 reporter interviews also indicated that many who go through a reporting process can develop a deep-seated distrust of their organisation. Issues likely to lessen, or even destroy, trust in the organisation were

- a perception of differential treatment of junior staff from senior staff when it came to dealing with reports of wrongdoing (associated with this was inconsistency in decision making)
- excessive loyalty to the organisation's reputation by senior managers that led to a hostile attitude to reporters
- a lack of communication or secretiveness—in particular, reporters not being allowed to talk about their report
- reporters feeling 'fobbed off' when a report was made
- reporters not being informed of procedures and their rights
- managers not standing up for the whistleblower
- issues being personalised by management
- line managers covering up for senior managers
- line managers perceived as being too frightened to take on the issues that have been raised in the reporting of wrongdoing.

These issues give some indication of the areas that organisations need to address if they wish to enhance their employees' trust that they take reporting of wrongdoing seriously and will act to protect reporters. While organisations might have reasonable whistleblowing procedures, in many organisations there is a common perception that those procedures are not followed. While managers might 'talk up' the procedures, when it came to action, some were prepared to ignore the policies and procedures. All these issues provide important reminders of the types of judgment that organisations can and should aim to avoid in addressing the following elements.

The issue of trust relates not only to the organisation itself but to the totality of what is known as the integrity system. This notion recognises that a number of government organisations like Ombudsman Offices, Anticorruption Commissions, Auditors General and Public Service Commissions form a complex interlocking network that promotes integrity in government. Annakin (2011, pp. 31-49) describes the evolution of this notion and its relevance to whistleblowing. She makes the observation that, in general, those organisations play an important role promoting trust among whistleblowers but that many organisations do not meet the expectations of whistleblowers. In particular Annakin found that many integrity agencies displayed shortcomings in the quality and amount of information published about their whistleblower protection processes (2011, p. 140).

A1. MANAGEMENT COMMITMENT

Checklist items

- Clear statements by senior management of the organisation's support for the reporting of wrongdoing through appropriate channels ('if in doubt, report'), including commitments to
  - take credible and appropriate action upon receipt of a whistleblowing report
  - remedy any confirmed wrongdoing
  - support whistleblowers.
- Commitment to the principles of whistleblowing among first and second-level managers, including
  - understanding of the benefits and importance of whistleblowing mechanisms
  - knowledge of and confidence in whistleblowing policies.
- Broad staff confidence in management responsiveness to whistleblowing.

For virtually all aspects of organisational activity, effective leadership leads to improvement of performance. This extends to encouraging employees to come forward with reports of wrongdoing and ensuring that the organisation protects them.

Leadership in the context of reporting wrongdoing comprehends

- actively engendering a culture supportive of whistleblowing and a culture of consistency, openness and transparency
- an emphasis on 'sorting out' bullying and harassment
- drawing the connection between whistleblowing, ethics and integrity
- resisting the temptation for leaders to simply look after their own position when under political pressure.

In the language of management theorists, these challenges expose the difference between transactional leadership and transformational leadership. Transactional leadership is where leaders guide or motivate their followers in the pursuit of established goals by clarifying role and task requirements. Transformational leaders go a step beyond this by inspiring individuals within the organisation to transcend their own self-interest for the greater good of the organisation (Robbins et al. 2008:432).

When considering a complex issue such as whistleblowing, the leadership style required is one that encourages line managers to put aside their personal concerns and to nurture, encourage and protect those employees who come forward with reports of wrongdoing.

In addition to the quantitative research, there was near unanimity among interviewees and the workshop participants that leadership or the 'tone at the top' was a crucial component of an effective reporting system. Many participants nominated leadership as being the most important factor in a successful whistleblowing system.

> [T]he cut-and-dry cases are managed quite clearly very well, very efficiently. It's the grey matters, the less clear cases that are difficult to manage because the managers who are trying to manage those situations are often subject to allegations themselves and bullying and stress associated with that. And so people avoid trying to manage situations.
> **Manager**

The 34 manager and case-handler interviewees were evenly divided in their opinions as to whether their organisation took a proactive approach to the reporting of wrongdoing (that is, actively encouraging reporting and having systems and procedures in place to handle reports and support reporters) or a reactive approach (that is, waiting until a report is made or adverse action occurs and then dealing with it).

The issue of leading by example was mentioned frequently. Many managers made the connection between acting promptly and properly with disclosures and encouragement to employees in making disclosures.

Managers need to consider that, not only does management provide a leadership role with regard to whistleblowing, but individual managers themselves could be the subject of investigations. The interviews revealed that this places quite a burden upon managers and those in the organisation who undertook the investigations.

Leadership on the issue of whistleblowing can also (potentially) come from the external accountability agencies. However, according to Annakin (2011, p 271), those external accountability agencies are not achieving the aims and objectives of the whistleblower protection legislation in their jurisdiction, she says that in the final analysis, it appears that accountability agencies failed to recognise the opportunities provided by whistleblowing cases for promoting organisational cultures that recognise the contribution of whistleblowers to the accountability. In this way, she says, they also failed to achieve the fundamental purpose of whistleblower legislation.

BACKING UP THE COMMITMENT WITH OBJECTIVES

A key finding of the research was that many employees reporting wrongdoing were sceptical about their organisation's commitment to the issue of protecting whistleblowers. An element of that scepticism was often the belief that nothing would be done in response to their report. This was consistent with the evidence that the most common reason for *not* reporting observed wrongdoing was the belief that the organisation would not do anything, even if a report was made (Wortley et al. 2008:72, Table 3.13).

Looking in more detail at issues of commitment.

- In their procedures, not all organisations committed themselves to encouraging reporting and protecting those employees who came forward with reports of wrongdoing, and practical elements to support those who had already reported occurred only sporadically in organisational whistleblower procedures (Roberts 2008:243, Table 10.8)

- The broader population of employees in a random sample was generally more positive about how their reports were handled than those participants who had been identified as reporters or internal witnesses. It should be noted that many of the former had reported informally whereas the latter group of participants included those for whom the matter was handled with some formality (Smith and Brown 2008:124)

- Where reports were made about wrongdoing undertaken by a specific person, the 58 reporter interviews suggested that reporters' assessments of commitment were likely to be dependent on whether wrongdoers were actually subject to some form of censure, as opposed to simply administrative improvements in the organisation.

From the examination of organisational procedures (see later in this section), it is clear that organisations are often better at setting up administrative mechanisms for the receipt of reports than following through and dealing with the issues that have been raised. That follow-through is a key factor in the credibility of an organisation's system for dealing with whistleblowing.

The setting of clear objectives can assist in improving an organisation's performance in this key area. At the level of individual report handling, organisations can improve their performance through the following.

- **Ensuring that a credible exploration of the report is made**. Reporters have an expectation that when they bring wrongdoing to notice, action will be taken to assess the accuracy of their claims. In some circumstances, this might involve a formal investigation (see Section C2), but even at an initial, more informal level (see Section B), or if no investigation is warranted, it is crucial that basic fact-finding and other management action short of formal investigation is professional, credible and accountable

- Having fully explored the background to the wrongdoing, **making a decision based upon the evidence to hand**

- Following through on that decision to **remedy any wrongdoing** that the reporter has brought to the attention of the organisation.

Managers' obligations vary with the many organisational structures that occur in the public sector. Organisations can range from very large departments of state with more than 100 000 employees to small local government or statutory bodies of less than 100 employees. It is important to be flexible and think in terms of not only the direct supervisor of the reporter but also—particularly in large organisations—perhaps two or three supervisory levels above the reporter.

Line managers wield a significant amount of authority over their employees. Most public sector organisations are hierarchically structured, making all employees largely dependent on their supervisors for career advancement and the day-to-day quality of their working environment. Public sector managers exercise wide employment discretions: they approve their subordinates' leave, they approve employees' transfer to other areas of the organisation, they make judgments about employees' competence and present (or misrepresent) those judgments to more senior managers. Because of these power relationships, employees who report wrongdoing often place themselves in a vulnerable situation when it comes to management.

Of employees surveyed who reported public interest wrongdoing, in 66 per cent of cases, the initial report was directly to their supervisor or their supervisor's immediate superior (Donkin et al. 2008:88, Table 4.1). Managers therefore play a very significant role in the whistleblowing process. It is up to those line managers, as the immediate recipient of most reports

- how they react to the report from their subordinate
- how they make initial judgments about the validity of the claims that are being presented to them
- how supportive (or non-supportive) they are of the reporter
- how knowledgeable they are about the organisational policies and processes
- how knowledgeable they are about the general principles of investigation and the need to determine the truth of the matter in a disinterested manner
- how committed they are to remedying any wrongdoing that is proven.

Managers themselves can be whistleblowers. Not only low-level employees report wrongdoing; employees of various levels or seniority may report (Wortley et al. 2008:58, Table 3.2). Consequently, someone who is a line manager to a junior employee can potentially be a reporter reporting to another level of line management.

Whistleblowing, like many other organisational activities, is affected by the attitudes that key players have towards the organisation. Managers tend to be much more positive about their organisation than the totality of employees (Mazerolle and Brown 2008:170, Table 7.1). In particular, they were more positive about the capacity of the organisations to properly deal with reports of wrongdoing and the protection of reporters. That difference is of such a degree that there could be some degree of overconfidence in managers' perceptions of the effectiveness of their own organisation's whistleblowing policies and procedures (Roberts 2008:254).

Figure 1.1 demonstrates the contrast between the attitudes of the reporters and those of the managers (and case-handlers) surveyed in the case-study agencies. While significant differences existed between the perceptions of managers and reporters in all organisations surveyed, the level of commitment shown by managers was largely consistent across these organisations.

Figure 1.1

Comparison of the perceptions of managers and internal witnesses of how committed their organisation is to 'dealing respectfully and properly with reporters'

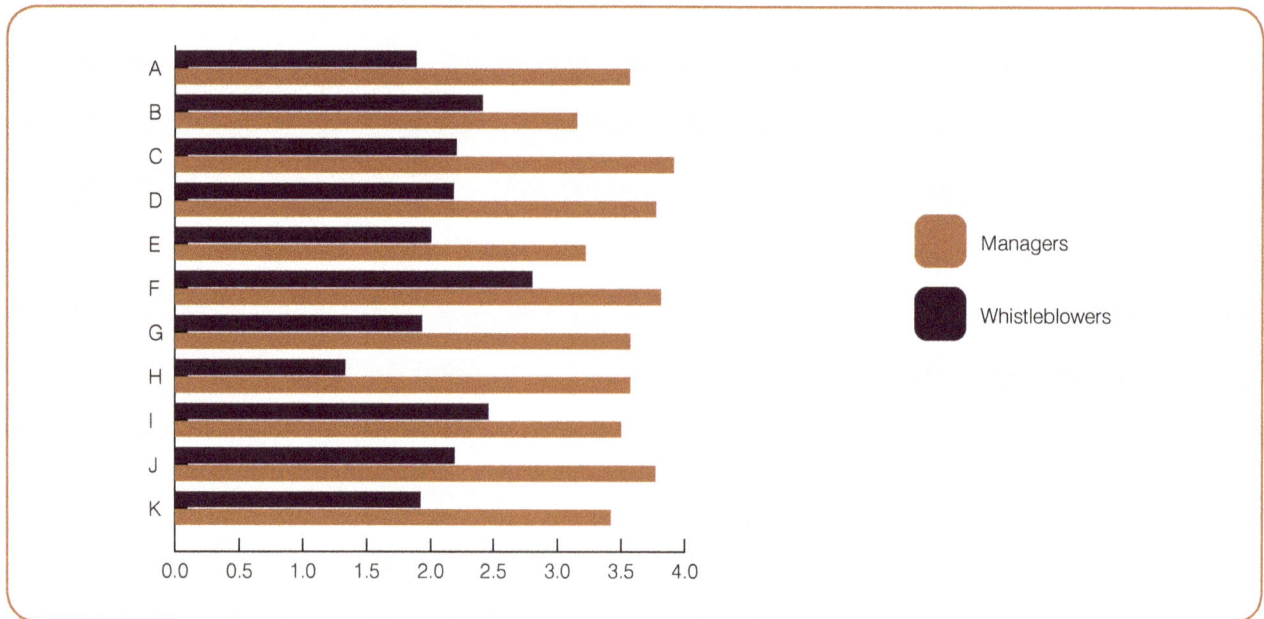

Note: As agencies were excluded if n < 5, only 11 of the 15 case-study agencies have been included.

Sources: Question 59 of the Case-Handler and Manager Survey; Question 61 of the Internal Witness Survey.

Nevertheless, the positive attitudes exhibited by managers provide a firm basis for organisations to move forward to meet the challenges discussed in this section. A key component of a successful approach to whistleblowing is the variety of attitudes that line managers themselves hold about those who come forward with reports of wrongdoing.

On balance, most managers and case-handlers recognise the value, importance and reliability of the organisational information that most whistleblowing provides (Brown et al. 2008b:45, Tables 2.12 and 2.13). In any organisation, however, there will remain a range of opinions about the issue.

In the case-study agencies, the 32 interviewed managers and case-handlers who expressed general opinions about whistleblowers broke down into roughly three groups: those who were positive towards reporters; those who were presumptively negative towards reporters, contrary to the overall weight of opinion (see box); and those who appeared to have a more balanced view, which was generally positive but included the need to balance reporters' needs with the interests of persons against whom allegations had been made. This analysis was based on unprompted expressions of opinion, rather than responses to specific questions.

Of the six case-handlers (either investigators or support staff) who expressed an opinion, five were positive towards reporters and one was negative towards reporters.

As a number of interviewees acknowledged, logic dictates that it is not a contradictory position for a line manager to be supportive of whistleblowers generally, yet to understand that persons against whom allegations are made also need support and protection.

We deal with so much stuff that's just nasty and vexatious and you know who the people are and they are able to hide behind the protected disclosure legislation. Because often, sadly, the complainant may be a person who is not performing terribly well in their job and they've got some overworked manager who is trying very hard to deal with their conduct and performance.

So then they make a whole lot of quite serious and largely unfounded allegations, they get protected disclosant status and then you're left with someone where everyone is terrified to put a performance program or whatever is needed in place.
Manager, Case-Study Agency

Particular issues for line managers are the following

- Reports are frequently about colleagues and superiors with whom the reporters have a close working relationship. For the line manager, those reports might well be about their own peers and colleagues. There is a temptation for the line manager to downplay the importance of the report so as to protect their own, or their colleagues', self-interest and credibility

- In large, complex organisations it is easy for line managers to shift the burden of responsibility onto some other part of the organisation. This could be the internal audit section, investigation unit or counselling staff engaged by the organisation

- Line managers have a capacity to influence more senior management levels of the organisation in a direct way and could exercise considerable discretion, potentially adverse or in favour of, the reporting subordinate

- Line managers also have the capacity to be passive in the reporting process in order to 'stay out of the firing line'. In larger, complex hierarchies, the line manager who fulfils organisational responsibilities is also placed in a difficult situation. This might not make the line manager as vulnerable as a reporter, but it is vulnerability nevertheless. Consequently, when organisations express commitment to supporting the reporters of wrongdoing, that support should extend to the direct recipient of the report.

It is not an easy task for organisations to ensure their line managers take risks in supporting reporters of wrongdoing. That is, however, what is being suggested here. Line managers should be encouraged to take on reports of wrongdoing as if they were their own, up to the point that it is clear, on the balance of probabilities, that the report has no substance and no further action is warranted. It is certainly within the power of individual organisations to create an organisational culture in which supporting reporters of wrongdoing is seen as an indication of superior management skills rather than a high-risk enterprise.

PRACTICAL ACTION

At the strategic level, there are a number of things that an organisation can do to demonstrate its commitment to encouraging reporting and the protection of those who report. These include

- clearly committing to protecting and respecting people who come forward with reports of whistleblowing and following that up with the sorts of action described below

- taking whistleblowing seriously at senior management level

- explicitly aiming for consistency in the application of policies and procedures

- setting targets within the organisation for increasing reporting rates, reducing inaction rates and increasing the proportion of reporters being actively managed by support staff

- committing to ensuring consistent responses from all management levels of the organisation (middle managers are the front line of the reporting process and they will need to exhibit management skills in assessing the validity of reports and understanding the formal recording processes of the organisation)

- where the responses to the reports are elevated to a formal investigation, committing to conducting such investigations in the most professional way (that is, resource costs for employing skilled investigators or, more likely, contracting in persons with those skills)

- at all levels in the organisation, taking the opportunity to learn from the unpleasant reports rather than papering over the cracks

- clearly stating and emphasising the difference between bullying and legitimate management action

- addressing problems rather than blaming people

- treating whistleblower complaints from staff with the same level of understanding as whistleblower complaints from outside the organisation by explicitly rejecting the approach of encouraging customer complaints but deeming whistleblower complaints from staff too hard

- where the investigation process, however formal or informal, results in a finding that action needs to be taken, decision makers within the organisation taking responsibility for ensuring that the action occurs.

Additionally, organisations should provide training and guidance for line managers in how they deal with their multiplicity of roles in the whistleblowing process, taking the following issues into account

- Line managers not only need to be familiar with the detail of the organisational procedures, they need to have some understanding of the importance of supporting and protecting reporters on a day-to-day basis. Such support and protection should be additional to, and not instead of, any dedicated resources that the organisation has in these areas

- Efforts are needed to ensure that line managers are more fully aware of the reality of their policies and procedures, notwithstanding that there might inevitably be a degree of scepticism among staff about those very policies and procedures and their implementation. Sensitivity to this issue should assist line managers in dealing effectively with reports of wrongdoing

- In dealing with their line managers, organisations need to be sensitive that reporting wrongdoing can place individual line managers in a potentially conflicting situation

- Organisations also need to be aware that individual line managers have the potential to cover up reports of wrongdoing that they might find embarrassing and might exhibit a human tendency to look after their own interests

- The biggest challenge in changing organisational culture towards whistleblowing will be getting line managers to accept that dealing effectively with reports of wrongdoing is an important part of their managerial responsibilities. Adopting a low profile should not be seen as an option.

A2. WHISTLEBLOWING POLICY

Checklist items

- Easy-to-comprehend whistleblowing policy, including guidance on procedures, relationship with other procedures, and legal obligations.

- Broad staff awareness of the whistleblowing program and policy, including their responsibility to report possible wrongdoing.

COMPREHENSIVE WHISTLEBLOWING POLICY

The research (Roberts 2008:245–60) confirmed that when it comes to whistleblowing, procedures in Australian public sector organisations

- are often not comprehensive, with only five of 175 agencies whose procedures were assessed in the project ranking as 'reasonably strong' against the requirements of the Australian Standard AS 8004-2003, *Whistleblower Protection Programs for Entities*

- vary considerably within and between jurisdictions

- the type of organisation appears to have little relevance to the comprehensiveness of standards

- issues related to the protection of internal witnesses are not well covered

> *[A]nd then they refer you to some other document and you're sitting there going, bloody hell, can't anybody just tell me what I'm supposed to do there in three simple sentences? So I'm sure it's there, but as a rule I don't know where to find it half of the time, and so then you're relying on others to find stuff for you and then once you get it, you go, well I don't actually know what that means because it's too bloody complex.*
> **Manager**

- many are poorly designed, and difficult to navigate and comprehend.

With regard to the ease of comprehension of the procedures, the following issues came to light.

- Many organisations provide their reporting procedures in too many places. A common pattern is for organisations to have one set of procedures outlining responsibilities for reporting in the code of conduct, another set of procedures for the process of reporting, and a further set of procedures dealing with investigation processes.

- There is a tendency to develop separate procedures closely aligned to different pieces of legislation rather than an integrated approach. Consequently, some procedures also read like an explanatory memorandum for a statute, with the legalistic nature of the language making comprehension difficult.

- A number of organisations demonstrated that it was possible to write procedures that were logical, user-friendly and used simply expressed language. These procedures stood out from the rest as being easy to read and understand.

Reporting procedures should be prepared for different audiences. Line managers, investigators and support personnel might need to have material that is more detailed and procedurally oriented. Potential reporters are going to want something that is simple and easy to read and which gives them confidence that they can proceed with their report.

An approach that some organisations adopted, and clearly found effective, was to have a 'user-friendly' guide for all staff with separate procedures specifically designed for line managers, investigators and support personnel. In Queensland, the Crime and Misconduct Commission, Ombudsman and Public Service Commission have promulgated separate guides for potential reporters and managers and for organisations (Crime and Misconduct Commission et al. 2009).

STAFF AWARENESS OF THE WHISTLEBLOWING PROGRAM

To be effective, whistleblowing policies and procedures need to be widely promulgated throughout the organisation. As shown in Table 1.1, across the 118 agencies that participated in the largest survey, reporters were significantly more likely to be aware of their organisation's procedures than non-reporters. The higher level of ignorance about whistleblowing procedures among those who did not report is a clear warning to organisations.

TABLE 1.1

Knowledge of procedures among employees who did or did not report

Category	Aware of procedures (%)	Stated that agency did not have procedures (%)	Did not know (%)
Reported observed wrongdoing (n = 2155)	82.3	3.0	14.7
Did not report (n = 3318)	71.4	4.2	24.4

Note: Significant at p < 0.001 level using Chi-square test.

Source: Questions 13 and 26 of the Employee Survey.

A key element of effective reporting procedures is the transmission to employees of knowledge and understanding of available legislative protections. This relationship is indicated by

- a strong correlation between employees' belief that they are covered by relevant legislation and the likelihood that they will blow the whistle

- the fact that employees who believe they are covered by legislation are also likely to believe that management's response to whistleblowing will be positive, including protection of their rights if they suffer reprisals

- a statistically significant relationship between employees' confidence in legislation and low employee inaction in response to observing wrongdoing (Roberts 2008:237–43, Tables 10.1, 10.2 and 10.7).

The challenges are, however, indicated by great variations in knowledge of legislation at the agency level, and the fact that managers often tend to be overly confident about the effectiveness of legislation alone to provide protection. These findings indicate that some organisations still have a long way to go in terms of making their employees aware of their legislative protection, and that this awareness is an important factor in promoting reporting and assuring employees that they will be protected.

For these reasons, staff awareness is a vital element of organisational commitment to whistleblowing. This was confirmed in the surveys of case-handlers (n = 253) and managers (n = 394) in the case-study agencies. When asked what were the most important things that could be changed within their organisation 'to ensure that wrongdoing in your organisation is reported more often and dealt with more effectively', the most commonly mentioned issues were training and education (15.4 per cent of case-handlers and 16 per cent of managers). 'Communication' was the second most commonly mentioned issue.

On the ground, there are a number of practical problems with the communication of reporting procedures.

- Whistleblowing procedures can get lost in the welter of policies and procedures that every public sector organisation must have in place to meet its governance obligations.

- The procedures are often not communicated within the organisation. Organisations frequently put their policies and procedures about reporting on their intranet, where staff find them very difficult to locate. This problem is aggravated when there are a large number of people within the organisation who do not have regular access to an organisational computer. One investigator made the observation that when employees are considering reporting wrongdoing, they are frequently under stress and highly emotional and this state of mind should be taken into account when thinking about communication strategies.

- Procedures are often not understood. A number of whistleblowers made the claim that they had accessed the agency procedures about which their immediate supervisors were not familiar, and guided them through the process.

- A comment made by some managers and many reporters was that their organisation's procedures were adequate on their face, but that in the handling of particular cases those procedures were not followed. One manager observed that comprehensive procedures on reporting wrongdoing encouraged reporters to trustingly come forward, only to find that the practical application of those procedures did not live up to their expectations.

A key issue that emerged from interviews was whether procedures for the reporting of wrongdoing should be simple and clear to read or comprehensive and sophisticated enough to deal with the multiplicity of situations that can arise in organisations in regards to the reporting of wrongdoing. The desirability of clarity in the procedures was a theme running through many of the interviews and many of the survey responses by managers and case-handlers.

A number of managers and case-handlers were of the view that agency procedures were too generic to deal with the complexity of the events that occurred. One manager described them as 'skeleton procedures'.

STAFF CONFIDENCE IN MANAGEMENT RESPONSIVENESS TO WHISTLEBLOWING

One of the key reasons employees do not report observed wrongdoing is a lack of confidence in the management response (Wortley et al. 2008:72, Table 3.13). As shown in Table 1.2, amongst employees the propensity to blow the whistle, confidence in whistleblowing legislation, awareness of agency whistleblowing procedures and trust in management are all closely associated.

TABLE 1.2

Comparison of awareness of procedures with whistleblowing propensity, confidence in legislation and trust in management's response to whistleblowing

	Whistleblowing propensity	Confidence in legislation	Attitude on how management would respond to report of wrongdoing
Aware of procedures (n = 5747)	3.88	3.21	3.37
Stated agency did not have procedures (n = 250)	3.44	2.78	2.90
Did not know (n = 1665)	3.38	2.82	3.10

Note: All significant at p < 0.001 level using Kruskal-Wallis H test.

Source: Questions 15, 17 and 18 of the Employee Survey.

> *The written policies and procedures could be improved. I don't think they adequately cover all of the scenarios that managers are presented with. How well they're implemented, I think, varies depending on the skill level of the manager involved in receiving a complaint or a notification and how well the investigation process is dealt with.*
> **Manager**

As well, employee awareness of organisational whistleblowing procedures and confidence in legislation are associated with the objectives of such procedures, such as encouraging reporting and protecting reporters (Roberts 2008:253, Tables 10.10 and 10.11).

EMPLOYEE ACCEPTANCE OF THEIR RESPONSIBILITY TO REPORT

The level of organisational commitment to a whistleblowing program can also be measured in terms of the level of staff acceptance that it is their responsibility to report public interest wrongdoing, rather than simply an exercise of a right. In many organisations—on their own account, at least 59 per cent of the 304 agencies who supplied information to the project—public sector employees are formally obliged to report wrongdoing. In parallel, a sense of ethical responsibility to report is the strongest reason provided by individuals for reporting wrongdoing (Wortley et al. 2008:71, Table 3.12).

On the best current evidence, a majority of employees (57 per cent of surveyed employees) feel they have had direct evidence of wrongdoing, but did not report it (Brown et al. 2008b:38, Figure 2.2). Even among organisations where there is a clear and publicised legal requirement to report (for example, in police services), managers are often aware of incidences where obvious wrongdoing has not been reported. While it is clear that having a legal obligation to report does not solve the issue of non-reporting, generating a more general sense of responsibility to report is central to the type of organisational climate—if supported by the 'tone at the top'—in which a whistleblowing program is likely to be effective.

PRACTICAL ACTION

To meet these challenges, organisations should

- develop comprehensive procedures that meet the requirements outlined in this guide

- clearly demonstrate their commitment to the reporting process in their procedures

- ensure their procedures devote sufficient coverage to the protection of internal witnesses

- ensure all procedures relating to reporting of wrongdoing are consistent and linked

- develop user-friendly procedures in plain language that are tailored to their specific audience (for example, investigators, line managers or reporters).

Additionally, in order to raise staff awareness of their whistleblowing program, increase staff confidence in management responsiveness to whistleblowing and ensure employees accept their responsibility to report wrongdoing, organisations need to

- think clearly about their communication strategy when developing their reporting procedures

- consult on their procedures with internal and external stakeholders—including staff, management and unions—to encourage all parties to consider the issues and provide constructive input to the reporting system

- have a multiplicity of media for communicating procedures

- have a range of levels of information, from very simple to comprehensive

- publicly acknowledge those staff members who have made valid disclosures as acting in the organisational interest

- find constructive ways, at the conclusion of major incidents, to ensure that any wrongdoing that has occurred in the organisation is acknowledged and openly discussed.

A3. RESOURCES

Checklist items

- Staffing and financial resources dedicated to implementation and maintenance of the program, commensurate with organisational size and needs.

- Specialised training for key personnel, including whistleblowing management issues as part of general induction and management training.

STAFFING AND FINANCIAL RESOURCES

There is no fixed formula as to what resources organisations should devote to whistleblowing programs. Realistically, the resourcing of a whistleblowing function within an organisation has to compete with a range of other governance priorities.

Nevertheless, those responsible for whistleblowing programs can often make good efficiency arguments for their programs. In the experience of some agencies, this includes quantifying the benefits of resources allocated to awareness raising and the training of managers, in comparison with the falling cost of investigations and other resource-intensive consequences flowing from wrongdoing uncovered too late, or failures in proactive support of reporters or management of workplace conflicts.

Many managers interviewed considered that the whistleblowing function within their organisation was adequately resourced. As with any other resourcing issue, there will be divided opinions, with some arguing that the resources dedicated to investigating and supporting reports of wrongdoing are misplaced.

A key question confronting all agencies is what scale of investment in a whistleblowing program—and particularly dedicated to whistleblower protection and support—is commensurate with the size and need of the agency. The questions of an appropriate model and the scale of a program depend on each organisation making a clear choice based on its own needs. This choice is discussed further in Section E1.

As will be discussed later in this guide, many employees come forward with reports of wrongdoing that are not handled by the formal whistleblowing functions within their organisation, and therefore might not be formally 'counted' for the purpose of determining agency case loads. Organisations should therefore avoid resourcing only to the known number of reports. A proactive approach to whistleblowing issues is also likely to encourage more people to seek the formal processes and support mechanisms. Many organisations need to make the shift from resourcing what they know is occurring to resourcing for what they think might be occurring, or is likely to occur.

SPECIALIST AND GENERAL TRAINING

Many managers and case-handlers nominate training and education in respect of dealing with whistleblowing as areas where organisations need improvement. Issues with training that were identified include

- while managers saw the need for training in respect of dealing with reports, it competed with other training requirements and there was a degree of management training fatigue
- training in regional areas of large organisations is more problematic than in central offices
- in many organisations, training is improving
- training in whistleblowing issues should be a part of a suite of general management competencies
- counselling skills were recognised as particularly important in managing whistleblowing.

In regards to the training of specialists, further issues were identified

- there exists a dearth of resources dedicated to specialised training in handling whistleblower reports (Brown and Wheeler 2008:306–8)

- the overall level of training in respect of investigation skills is not very high

- there is inconsistency in the level and type of training of investigators, with little training provided in circumstances where a much higher level could reasonably be expected (Mitchell 2008:191–7).

PRACTICAL ACTION

In considering training relating to whistleblowing, organisations can give attention to

- the current adequacy of skills within the organisation in respect of investigations and support

- including training on whistleblowing policies and procedures in general management training

- specific training for the investigation of reprisals.

A4. EVALUATION AND ENGAGEMENT

Checklist items

- Regular evaluation and continual improvement in the program.
- Positive engagement on whistleblowing issues with external integrity agencies, staff associations and client groups.

EVALUATION AND CONTINUAL IMPROVEMENT

As with any program within an organisation, it is necessary to regularly evaluate its effectiveness. While noting that most public sector organisations have standardised procedures for the evaluation of programs, the following would be desirable

- a formalised system for recording all reports of wrongdoing, their outcome, and details of any support provided to the reporter or a person who is the subject of allegations

- an estimate of the resources allocated to particularly difficult and complex cases

- a regular survey of the attitude of managers towards their organisation's whistleblowing policy and process

- a regular survey of employee awareness of the whistleblowing policies and procedures, and trust in these procedures.

It is also suggested that organisations ensure their whistleblowing program is included in the organisation's governance structure, and embedded in other organisational systems (see Section E4). This will also ensure that evaluation of the effectiveness of the program would be subject to regular scrutiny by an audit committee or its equivalent.

EXTERNAL ENGAGEMENT ON WHISTLEBLOWING ISSUES

A final important indicator of organisational commitment is external engagement with key stakeholders on whistleblowing issues, including for the purposes of evaluating the program (as discussed above). A good relationship with all relevant integrity agencies is an important element of organisational commitment to reporting of wrongdoing.

Many managers and case-handlers interviewed were strongly in favour of a greater role for external oversight agencies, considering that

- external agencies could take an independent perspective on issues

- most external agencies have investigative resources not available to organisations, including stronger statutory powers; consequently, it was recognised that the quality of investigations undertaken by those external agencies was far higher

- associated with the above issue, when matters are reported externally and investigated by an external organisation, internal witnesses might be more likely to provide useful information so as to make the investigation more comprehensive.

When taking these responses into consideration, however, the following qualifications should be considered. First, as has been noted elsewhere, most reporters prefer to do so internally and only the minority will make an external report. Consequently, many of the managers interviewed did not have much experience of cases that had been handled by an external agency.

Second, every jurisdiction studied had a multiplicity of external agencies and some organisations working in specific areas could have quite a number that they were answerable to. Their functions were quite distinct, although there is inevitably some overlap.

Consequently, when managers were making comments about external agencies they could be referring to

- ombudsman's offices or anti-corruption agencies, which have significant powers and investigative resources

- public sector management agencies, which performed more of an oversight than an investigative role

- other external agencies, which acted more like regulators for a specific sector, looking at issues and making recommendations as to how the organisation could improve its administration.

Attitudes towards the involvement of external agencies in reporting programs were mixed. Managers acknowledge the efficacy of having a skilled, detached authority overseeing the process. This is tempered by views that some reporters can go 'forum shopping', looking for a recipient authority that will take a more sympathetic view than their own organisation.

When reports are received by or referred to an external agency, they are often referred back to the organisation for handling, with the external agency to be informed of the outcome at some stage for monitoring purposes. Most interviewees accepted the efficacy of this approach with some resentment that the organisation is taking the burden of responsibility. This acceptance was not reflected in reporter interviews, where referral back to their own organisation was frequently characterised by reporters as the external agency not fulfilling its proper role.

It is clear that governments should have at least one coordinating integrity agency with the statutory authority and capacity to oversee and respond readily to the range of issues that the reporting of wrongdoing raises for agencies (Brown and Wheeler 2008:310). This is an important principle for any best-practice public interest disclosure regime (Brown et al. 2008a:282–7), and is a recommendation recently accepted by many governments, included in amendments to the NSW *Public Interest Disclosure Act 2010* and foreshadowed by the Commonwealth Government (Australian Government 2010).

While this is a vital element, it will, however, most often remain the case that responsibility for dealing with the matter, as well as supporting and protecting reporters, *does* lie with the organisation in which the wrongdoing occurred. As noted in Section A1, managers and supervisors—often more than external agencies—are well placed to identify the risks that contribute to the misconduct occurring, take the opportunity to learn from the complaint, and subsequently improve the ethical climate of their workplace. Often, the role of external agencies can be best fulfilled by supporting organisations in meeting this challenge, closely monitoring whether minor reports of wrongdoing are dealt with appropriately by organisations, and investigating only the most serious cases.

An organisation can demonstrate its commitment to whistleblowing most effectively by demonstrating openly to outside agencies that it is taking responsibility for dealing with wrongdoing by its own employees, as well as supporting and protecting its own reporters.

PRACTICAL ACTION

Organisations can take a number of steps to ensure the continual improvement of their whistleblowing program and relationship with external agencies.

- Evaluation of the effectiveness of a whistleblowing program should be conducted with the same rigour and detail that organisations use to evaluate other programs. This should include the setting of key performance indicators, such as the number of reports received or the proportion of investigations that result in substantiation/ action being taken/support provided to reporters or subject officers.

- As has been indicated by the research, there is some disjunction between management perceptions of the success of their programs and the attitudes of reporters. Organisations are urged to go beyond normal evaluation practices and to survey staff about their reporting experience, and their trust in management to handle their reports sympathetically and effectively.

- Organisations should liaise with external agencies dealing with whistleblowing reports professionally and sympathetically. Those agencies, in the course of fulfilling their functions, frequently develop useful insights into how the organisation is operating, which can be of benefit to management. Where possible, organisations should meet regularly with those external agencies and, where practicable, encourage them to participate in awareness-raising programs related to the reporting process.

SAMPLE POLICIES AND PROCEDURES

The policy should be an integral part of the organisation's commitment to developing and supporting a culture in which the reporting of wrongdoing and systemic failure is considered to be a positive action to promote integrity, accountability and good management.

No particular form of words is provided because an essential part of committing to certain values and developing a statement of such values is that it is meaningful and relevant to each agency and not just adopting a pro forma approach.

The principal audience for the policy is the agency's staff and the language should reflect this. Managers at all levels should also be made aware of the policy, not only as potential reporters, but as potential recipients of reports.

The policy should be

- a manifestation of the commitment of the organisation to high standards of ethical and accountable conduct and confirmation that the organisation does not tolerate corrupt conduct, maladministration or waste of public money

- in accordance with relevant codes of ethics/conduct that have been promulgated within the jurisdiction/organisation

- specifically addressing the obligations under the relevant public interest disclosure legislation
- specifically and formally endorsed by the CEO
- explicitly expressing the belief that staff who come forward and report wrongdoing are acting as exemplary organisational citizens and assisting in promoting integrity, accountability and good management.

The policy should make specific commitments to

- engender an organisational climate in which staff will feel comfortable and confident about reporting wrongdoing
- encourage any staff member to come forward if they have witnessed what they consider to be wrongdoing within the organisation
- respond to reports in a way that will protect the identity of the staff member reporting wrongdoing, wherever possible and appropriate
- protect the staff member who made the report from any adverse action taken as a result
- protect the dignity, wellbeing, career interests and good name of all persons involved
- deal with the report thoroughly and impartially and, where some form of wrongdoing has been found, take appropriate action to rectify it
- keep the staff member informed of progress and the outcome
- while encouraging staff members to report within the organisation, respect any decision to report wrongdoing outside the organisation, provided that reporting outside the organisation is legal and valid
- ensure that managers at all levels in the organisation understand the benefits to the organisation of whistleblowing, are familiar with the policies and sensitive to the needs of those who report wrongdoing
- provide adequate resources, both financial and human, are made available to
    - protect and support those who make reports
    - provide relevant training for key personnel
    - effectively investigate reports
    - properly manage any workplace issues that the reports identify or create
    - remedy any wrongdoing that has been established.

B.

FACILITATING REPORTING

I think, in general, people in my organisation don't want to report. They're afraid of reporting, they are afraid of victimisation and I think that those fears are valid. I think there's a lot of evidence when somebody makes a complaint that they then get victimised by that. So I think for that reason, if anyone decides to make a complaint they tend to go straight to [the integrity agency]…They tend to go outside because they feel that they might actually be a bit more protected than going internally.
Manager

Encouraging the reporting of wrongdoing is the first major objective of any whistleblowing program. Although a considerable amount of reporting of possible wrongdoing by public employees occurs, there is considerable evidence of the reticence of employees to report, or to do so in a timely fashion. Some of this reticence might relate to deficiencies in formal systems, including the complexity and lack of comprehensiveness of formal whistleblowing legislation. These factors are barriers to the establishment of an 'if in doubt, report' culture within organisations and the general public sector (Brown et al. 2008a:261–8).

More pervasive problems relate to the reporting climate within organisations, where the bulk of evidence of wrongdoing is identified but where employees and organisation members can face natural disincentives to speak up. Disincentives to reporting can range from a desire to protect one's career and avoid workplace conflict to uncertainty over the seriousness of the problem, fear of reprisal, and unwillingness to 'rock the boat' or challenge friends and colleagues.

TABLE 2.1

Managers' and case-handlers' views on how well their organisation encourages reporting

Item	Case-handlers (n = 340)		Managers (n = 535)	
	Mean	SD	**Mean**	SD
Success of organisation in encouraging reporting of wrongdoing (1 = not at all, 5 = extremely)	**3.03**	0.97	**3.20**	0.87

Source: Question 61 of the Case-Handler and Manager Survey.

Table 2.1 is one indication that managers and case-handlers in the case-study agencies were ambivalent about their organisations' success in encouraging the reporting of wrongdoing. Also indicative was a disturbingly high rate of respondents (28.6 per cent) who witnessed wrongdoing that they considered serious but did not report it (Brown et al. 2008b:48).

The final indication of these problems is illustrated in Figure 2.1, which shows the case-study agencies ranked by inaction rate (that is, the proportion of respondents who saw very or extremely serious wrongdoing that they did not report or deal with themselves and they did not know of others reporting). While a majority of the agencies were at, or below, the national mean, one-third were above it, confirming the varying degrees of success of the case-study agencies in establishing a successful whistleblowing program at the time of the research.

The most basic and practical element in an effective reporting system is clarity, including the need to precisely identify who is covered, what is covered, and how the organisation should coordinate its handling of different types of reports. More complex elements include ensuring the availability of multiple reporting pathways, whereby employees may bring forward reports of wrongdoing either to their line managers—currently the recipients of the overwhelming majority of whistleblowing disclosures—or to alternative reporting points within the organisation such as an integrity or ethical standards unit or externally to agencies such as ombudsman's offices and anti-corruption bodies (Donkin et al. 2008:88, 89, Table 4.1 and Table 4.2).

FIGURE 2.1

Inaction rates across the case-study agencies

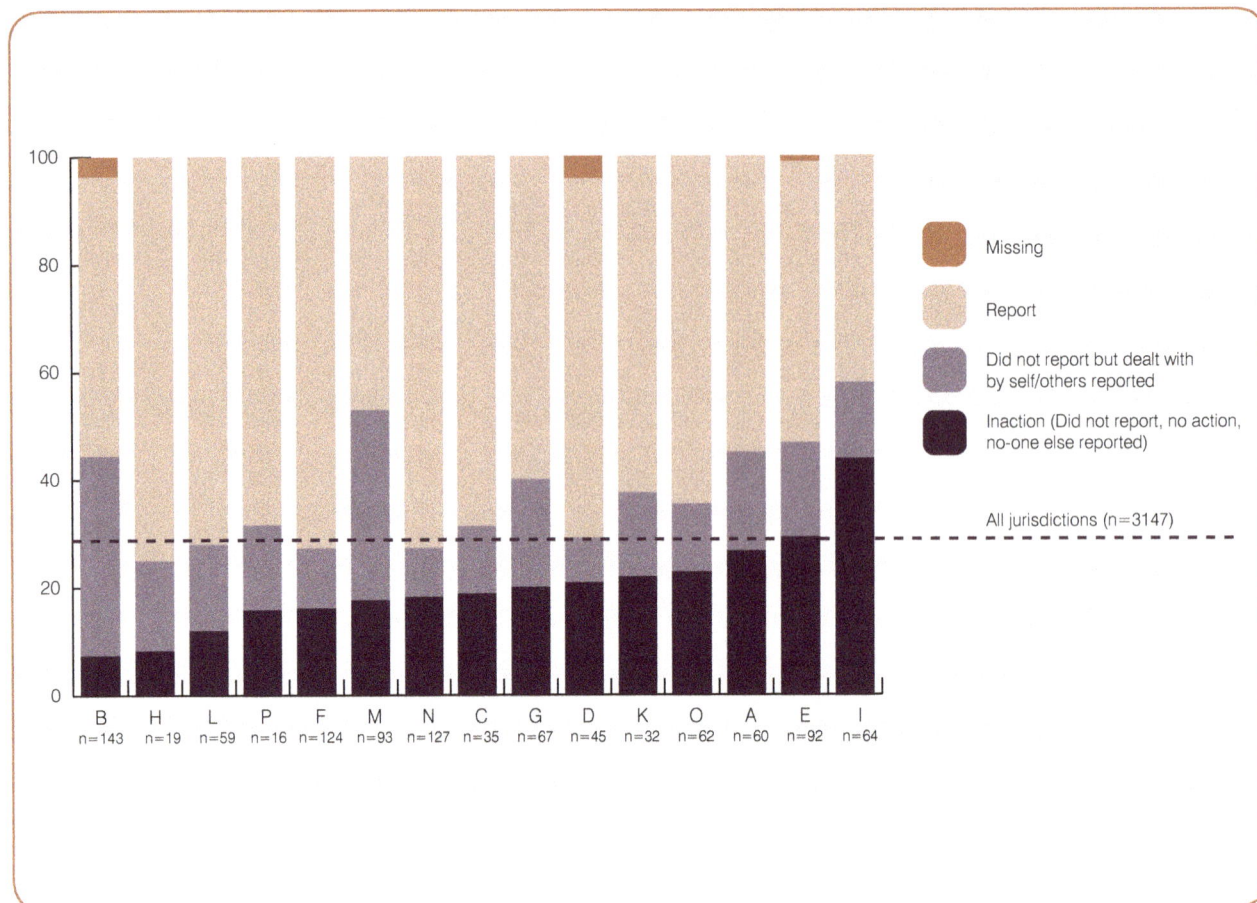

Organisations are urged to advise employees that these bodies are alternative recipients of reports of wrongdoing. The need for organisations to maintain close and positive working relations with these organisations has already been discussed. A final key component in encouraging reporting is for the organisation to have credible mechanisms for offering anonymity, backed up by realistic undertakings of confidentiality, for reporters.

The awareness and accessibility of these alternative pathways might be vital to not only maximising the likelihood of employees reporting but also to ensuring that disclosures are properly handled, and the whistleblower is effectively supported. Where employees believe that making a report of wrongdoing will immediately spread through the informal gossip grapevine within the organisation, it is unlikely that they will come forward to report wrongdoing.

A final key component in encouraging reporting is for the organisation to have credible mechanisms for allowing anonymous reporting, backed up by realistic undertakings of confidentiality. While this raises the first of many complex issues in the management of disclosures, the research suggests it is a worthy objective that every organisation should aim for.

B1. WHO MAY REPORT WRONGDOING?

Checklist item

- Clear and comprehensive approach to including all key categories of organisation members (for example, employees, contractors, employees of contractors, volunteers) in the program.

IDENTIFYING WHO NEEDS TO BE INCLUDED IN THE WHISTLEBLOWING PROGRAM

While the coverage of whistleblowing policies and procedures might be shaped by the legislative system in which the organisation is operating (Donkin et al. 2008:83–108), it is also open to agencies to set many of their own parameters for those organisation members that the whistleblowing program is intended to encourage and attract.

Some whistleblowing legislation recognises that 'any person', including members of the public, may make a public interest disclosure. For example, the *Public Interest Disclosure Act 2010* (Qld) provides that *any person* may make a disclosure in relation to reprisal or dangers to the health or safety of a person with a disability or the environment, but that only *public officers* may disclose official misconduct, maladministration, waste of public funds or danger to public health or safety. In fact, this approach is not consistent with accepted definitions of a whistleblower as an 'organisation member'. Nevertheless, it is important for organisations to identify those classes of complainant crucial to the agency for whom the risk of detrimental action represents a major barrier to disclosure of wrongdoing.

Most organisations focus upon serving employees in terms of their whistleblowing policies and procedures. Some organisations, where there is a significant amount of work undertaken by contractors and subcontractors, should focus upon their needs as well. Similarly, a range of volunteers and particular types of 'at risk' clients might need to be able to qualify for an equivalent type of protection and support as employees.

Most policies that were examined as a part of this research project (Roberts 2008) adequately defined the coverage of their whistleblowing policies and procedures. Interviews with managers and case-handlers, however, revealed an overwhelming focus upon current employees. Training of managers should therefore emphasise that they might receive reports from other sources and the implications of this.

PRACTICAL ACTION

It is usual for the definition of coverage in whistleblowing policies and procedures to follow the relevant legislation. Organisations are encouraged to look beyond the generic categorisation in the legislation and attempt to identify if they have any stakeholders or clients who might be in a position to identify wrongdoing and need protection were they to do so. Care should be taken to clearly identify the degree of protection that can be given in these circumstances.

This issue is dealt with in the sample procedures set out below.

B2. WHAT SHOULD BE REPORTED?

Checklist items

- Clear procedures and advice to staff on
    - the types of wrongdoing that should be reported
    - appropriate reporting points for all different types of wrongdoing (including grievances as opposed to public interest disclosures)
    - the level of information required/desired in a report.
- Clear advice that staff
    - are not protected from the consequences of their own wrongdoing by reporting it, nor for deliberately providing false or misleading information
    - may nevertheless seek and be granted immunity from consequences from their own less serious wrongdoing, when reporting other more serious wrongdoing.

DEFINING REPORTABLE WRONGDOING

Legislation might help define or limit the degree of discretion that agencies have in defining the types of wrongdoing that should be reported. In drafting policies and procedures, organisations should have a mix of defined issues that may be reported upon, but also a broader 'catch-all' provision, in keeping with the 'if in doubt, report' message.

The sample procedures also contain a suggestion on how organisations can deal with this issue.

One benefit to organisations having a broad 'catch-all' provision relating to the types of wrongdoing that may be reported is the collection of valuable intelligence about issues that might, on a case-by-case basis, appear to be minor but indicate a serious pattern when looked upon in aggregate. For example, where an organisation receives a large number of reports about minor fraud, this could indicate a more serious, systemic problem.

It is undesirable for any type of wrongdoing to be so closely defined that line managers and reporters believe that an issue falls outside the policies and procedures on a technicality. The bottom line is that organisations are better positioned if they make decisions on a day-to-day basis about whether or not a particular issue should be dealt with as a whistleblowing report rather than having it set out in some form of formal procedure.

One of the implications of this approach is the added responsibility upon line managers to give feedback to reporters if an issue is determined not to be worthy of further action. Ideally, that feedback, along with the reasons for the determination, should be provided to the reporter as soon as possible after the decision.

REPORTING POINTS FOR ALL WRONGDOING TYPES

There is considerable complexity in unravelling employment-related grievances and public interest wrongdoing (Brown et al. 2008b:49–51). In the research, the list of issues that could be reported was long and ranged from serious public interest matters, such as corruption and perverting the course of justice, through to workplace grievances, including personnel actions and bullying. Some workplace grievances, particularly those involving management, can become so endemic and destructive that they also become a public interest issue.

The category of personnel and workplace grievances was the largest of the seven categories of wrongdoing nominated by employees, five of which were clearly public interest issues. As outlined in Table 2.2 in the first report, 48.7 per cent of respondents to the Employee Survey (n = 7663) reported that they had observed wrongdoing that could be categorised as personnel or workplace grievances, and 22.2 per cent (n = 1702) indicated that the wrongdoing was somewhat, very or extremely serious. (It should be noted that respondents were able to nominate more than one type of wrongdoing that they had observed.)

Distinguishing between employment-related grievances and public interest wrongdoing is vital for organisations given the significant proportion of reporters who experience an employment-related grievance at the same time that they report wrongdoing. Of the 214 respondents to Question 23 of the Internal Witness Survey (including those who reported a workplace grievance), 41.6 per cent indicated that at the time they reported wrongdoing they were experiencing conflict or serious disagreement with their managers or supervisors. Conversely, 21.6 per cent (n = 74) of respondents who reported only public interest wrongdoing stated that they had a disagreement with their managers or supervisors at the same time. Interviews with reporters indicated that not only were public interest issues coexisting with personnel issues but also many reporters did not distinguish between the two.

The coincidence of different issues has the potential to complicate the way in which an organisation responds to disclosures. Figure 2.2 provides a good example of the type of advice that can be given to employees to help them understand that different types of wrongdoing might have different reporting points, and be handled in different ways. The crucial thing confirmed by the quantitative research and the workshops is the need for agencies to provide for all wrongdoing types, whether through coordinated advice about the relevant internal reporting points or through a 'one-stop shop' approach, such as a general, all-purpose complaints and disclosure line, as employed by some case-study agencies.

Irrespective of where disclosures are received, careful assessment is desirable to ensure that the different elements of a disclosure are all dealt with appropriately. The problems raised by this issue—especially in light of the fact that the bulk of disclosures is received by supervisors and line managers—are discussed in detail in Section C1.

FIGURE 2.2

Sample advice to public employees regarding reporting points

So you think you may have seen something in your workplace that shouldn't be happening?

Not sure what to do about it?

STOP AND ASK YOURSELF

Depending on the type of wrongdoing or danger that you are concerned about, there are different people you can, and should, talk to.

What kind of information do you have?

IS IT ABOUT BULLYING OR HARASSMENT?

Consult your organisation's bullying or harassment policy and talk to your manager or Human Resources (HR) section. If the matter is serious enough, it may be a public interest disclosure.

Keep reading.

IS IT A GRIEVANCE OR IS IT ABOUT WORKPLACE CONFLICT?

Consult your organisation's grievance policy and talk to your manager, HR section or union.

IS IT A WORKPLACE HEALTH AND SAFETY (WH&S) ISSUE?

Consult your organisation's WH&S policy and talk to your manager or WH&S officer.

IS IT ABOUT OFFICIAL MISCONDUCT OR A REPRISAL?

It may be a public interest disclosure.

Keep reading.

IS IT ABOUT MALADMINISTRATION OR A WASTE OF PUBLIC FUNDS?

It may be a public interest disclosure.

Keep reading.

IS IT ABOUT DANGER TO PUBLIC HEALTH OR SAFETY, THE HEALTH OR SAFETY OF A PERSON WITH A DISABILITY OR THE ENVIRONMENT?

It may be a public interest disclosure.

Keep reading.

IS IT A COMBINATION OF THE ABOVE?

You may have concerns about bullying or workplace conflict as well as information that may be a public interest disclosure.

Keep reading.

NOT SURE?

Seek advice from your manager, another senior manager, your HR section or one of the organisations listed on pp. 28–30.

Source: Crime and Misconduct Commission et al. (2009).

LEVEL OF INFORMATION REQUIRED/DESIRED BEFORE REPORTING

Organisational policies as well as their practical implementation have to steer the difficult path between encouraging employees to bring forward genuine concerns and avoiding setting such a low threshold of reporting that line managers are swamped with unfounded suspicions.

Setting the bar too high means that reports are discouraged because the reporter believes that a high level of proof is required before making a report. It might also jeopardise a proper investigation, or increase the risk of reprisal or other conflict, by causing the employee to try to investigate the matter themselves in order to gather 'harder' evidence before coming forward. A suggestion for how this issue can be dealt with is covered in the suggested procedures.

INVOLVEMENT OF REPORTERS IN WRONGDOING

The credibility of the whistleblowing program depends on it not being used by employees as a self-protective strategy in relation to their own wrongdoing or workplace failures. This is important not only for organisational justice, but also because misinterpretation of the motives of reporters can undermine the scheme. Analysis of the interviews indicated that most managers in the agencies studied were not influenced by negative stereotypes of whistleblowers and did not think that whistleblowers were overwhelmingly vexatious, or simply seeking to protect themselves by making to damage others. The interviews also confirmed, however, that some do hold this view and that where such a negative view is prevalent, it is likely that there will be discord and reprisal as a result of the report.

It should be clearly stated and understood in the whistleblowing policy of the organisation that the act of reporting does not necessarily protect the reporter from the consequences of their own wrongdoing. This is also usually the legislative position.

The separate but related issue of a reporter providing deliberately false or misleading information is one that is often mentioned in legislation. If this is the case then organisational policies need to reflect the intent of the legislation. If it is not covered in legislation, this issue needs to be dealt with along the lines suggested in the sample procedures below.

IMMUNITY FOR REPORTERS

There might be situations where a reporter comes forward with a report of serious wrongdoing in which they have some minor involvement. There might also be situations where an employee is aware that if they disclose wrongdoing by others, or about the organisation, they can anticipate a likely 'payback' complaint against them by other employees or managers—which might have some basis—and therefore be deterred from reporting.

Such payback complaints (and even 'pre-emptive strike' complaints) against whistleblowers or possible whistleblowers do arise. Examination of the reporter interview transcripts (n = 58) indicated that 'payback' reporting occurred with seven reporters—five initiated by the reporter and two against reporters by other parties. In these circumstances, agencies must be especially careful not to send a message through the organisation regarding its treatment of whistleblowers that submitting a report makes the reporter 'fair game' for payback complaints. This will risk creating an environment in which reporting becomes a tit-for-tat retaliatory battleground.

To address payback complaints, organisations could provide in their procedures that, in *some* circumstances, they may exercise discretion not to proceed with action against the reporter as a result of their own action. Again, a suggested form of words is provided in the sample procedures below.

PRACTICAL ACTION

Organisations are encouraged to ascertain whether any functions particular to their organisation need to be added to their list of defined reportable wrongdoing, with the proviso that caution needs to be taken with noting the limitations on protection (that is, that it is not provided for in legislation).

Organisations are urged to be as flexible as possible in their practices and procedures when it comes to determining the level of information required prior to making a report of wrongdoing.

Most public sector organisations in Australia have restrictions on the unauthorised disclosure of information. While employees should be made aware of their obligations, care should be taken to distinguish between unauthorised disclosure and reporting of wrongdoing. It should not be assumed that employees can easily make this distinction.

B3. MULTIPLE REPORTING PATHWAYS

Checklist items

- Clear advice on *to whom* and *how* whistleblowing reports should be made, including
  - *internal* reporting paths
  - *alternatives* to direct line reporting (that is, guidance on when staff should consider reporting outside the normal management chain)
  - *external* reporting paths, including external (contracted) hotlines and relevant regulatory or integrity agencies, and when these should be approached in the first instance.
- Clear advice regarding disclosures to the media.

When employees report wrongdoing, they overwhelmingly do it to a limited category of participants (primarily immediate supervisors or other senior managers). Of public interest reporters, 87 per cent indicated that their initial reports went to four categories of recipients: supervisors (65.7 per cent), senior managers (15 per cent), peer support officers (3.5 per cent) and CEOs (3.4 per cent). Another 10 categories of recipients received lesser proportions of reports (n = 835) (Donkin et al. 2008:88, Table 4.1). The range of *potential* recipients for reports nominated by organisations is quite broad, with CEOs nominated as authorised recipients of reports by 85.5 per cent of agencies (n = 304), any manager more senior than the reporter by 37.5 per cent, any senior person the reporter has confidence in by 29.3 per cent, and internal ethical standards/investigation unit or officer by 23.6 per cent. Another 12 categories of recipients were mentioned in Question 14 of the Agency Survey, and agencies could nominate more than one category of recipients.

Superficially, this pattern would appear to indicate that a wide range of potential recipients is unnecessary. Logically, however, even if reports are going to a very small number of recipients, the wide variety of circumstances of reporting would indicate that a multiplicity of reporting pathways is needed. In practice, it is most desirable that a high degree of redundancy be built in to reporting systems. The big challenge for agencies is that the most common reporting pathway—the line manager—is probably the most difficult to manage in terms of ensuring consistency and adherence to agency procedures and policies.

One indicator that suggests some agencies do not take a sufficiently flexible approach is the response to Question 20 of the Agency Survey; organisations (n = 304) were asked whether they would accept oral reports from staff: 72.7 per cent said 'yes', but 22.7 per cent said 'no' (with 4.3 per cent not responding). Of those agencies that accepted oral reports, the estimated percentage of reports that were oral was 10.3. Internal pathways not only need to be clearly identified by organisations, the recipients of reports need to be able to deal with the reporting event in a nuanced and flexible way.

INTERNAL PATHWAYS: HOW REPORTS ARE MADE

Knowing that the overwhelming majority of reporters currently choose to go to a line manager as their first point of contact, internal agency procedures ideally should be structured in a way that recognises that reality. In looking at best practice in reporting, it is useful to focus upon some of the more administrative and technical issues on how reports are made, including who receives reports.

A commonly mentioned pathway for whistleblowing reports is anonymous hotlines. Internal hotlines were seen by managers to have particular benefits even though only a few reporters appear to use that avenue of reporting (Donkin et al. 2008:88, Table 4.1).

Recipients of reports face a difficult task, needing to stand above personal interest and look to the long-term benefit for the organisation while at the same time dealing responsibly and professionally with a reporter who is likely to be under considerable stress. Again, a major issue for organisations is that so many of their staff, sometimes at relatively junior levels, might not have the skills to conduct careful assessment of reports.

EXTERNAL REPORTING PATHWAYS

Yeah, I think the hotline's important because I think the hotline can take the emotion out of it. Because I think a line manager gets the report of wrongdoing and, because of things that have happened in the last five or six years, they tend to think, how can I support myself in this? How can I make sure I don't get burned by all of this, rather than thinking of, well, what am I really hearing here? Whereas the hotline tends to be—they're looking at the issue only of what's been reported. They haven't got an emotional bank in this or anything.
Manager

Only a small proportion of reporters of wrongdoing utilise external pathways for reporting (Donkin et al. 2008:90). Overall, agency procedures do not define external pathways as comprehensively as internal pathways (Roberts 2008:246). For the reasons discussed above, however, organisations are urged to clearly define external pathways and make them available to staff.

Reporters might fear retribution if they report internally (Wortley et al. 2008:72, Table 3.13). The decision to go to an external authority takes the report to another level of formality and can be a source of considerable confusion, tension and anxiety. In relation to making reports external to the organisation

- even though the overwhelming majority of respondents to the Employee Survey had access to external reporting pathways, many reporters were not aware of their rights to seek review by an external party

- some reporters are reluctant to refer matters to an external authority for fear of being penalised

- there is frequent misunderstanding about the niceties of the different roles of external reporting agencies, with reporters being unaware that integrity agencies perform different functions, even though many of them overlap

- some reporters do not seek to report externally because of preconceptions about particular integrity agencies, however, these preconceptions (usually, that nothing will be done) appear to be based upon gossip and rumour

- there was frustration that some external organisations do not accept reports because they do not meet the formal requirements of the organisations and thus appear to be uncaring and unnecessarily legalistic and bureaucratic. This finding is in accordance with the observations made by Annakin (2011, p 269).

There is an assumption that when reporters approach external agencies they do so on a formal basis. When it comes to communication with external agencies, however, reporters do use informal channels of communication in order to get some indication of how their report will be accepted. This use of the 'grapevine' can have a clear advantage for reporters, but there are considerable disadvantages in that informal oral approaches are subject to misinterpretation.

WHICH PATH: UP THE LINE, INTERNAL OR EXTERNAL?

From the perspective of managers (and case-handlers), the involvement of external agencies in the reporting of whistleblowers can be seen in a positive light. External agencies have the resources, skills, powers and an independent perspective, which, overall, can be of benefit in the handling of the report.

External reporting agencies often, however, refer matters back to the reporter's home organisation for detailed investigation and/or to be dealt with in other ways, and this can cause the perception of problems. While managers and case-handlers recognised the administrative efficacy of this process, the downsides were frequently commented upon. One particular downside was that where a case had been referred back to the home organisation that organisation then had to approach the reporter to obtain more information about the report. This situation is difficult because the reporter has already taken a quite deliberate decision to report externally and sometimes resents that the report has ended up in a home organisation rather than being taken and dealt with by the external agency.

Another source of frustration with the process of referral back of reporting cases is the difference that it frequently highlights between the priorities of the external agency and of the referring organisation. That difference of opinion over priority will often be a source of frustration to the reporter, who will have clear views about the priorities that the report should be afforded.

The findings above are confirmed by Annakin (2011). She found that:

- whistleblowers chose to report to an external agency not so much out of any explicit trust but because the external agency represented the 'last resort' for their reporting process (p. 179);

- the fact that those external agencies tended to rely upon departmental investigations rather than conducting an independent investigation was a matter of annoyance to the whistleblowers. As Annakin says (p. 268), ' whistleblowers were surprised, and in some cases horrified, to find that accountability agencies did not conduct independent investigations of their disclosures, even when the likelihood of wrongdoing was confirmed'; and

- many whistleblowers were of the view that those external agencies were more interested in finding ways to refuse disclosures then investigating them. Following on from this, she found that it was unusual for an outcome that was different or better achieved through a reporting to an external agency (p. 269).

> *I think, in general, people in my organisation don't want to report. They're afraid of reporting, they are afraid of victimisation and I think that those fears are valid. I think there's a lot of evidence when somebody makes a complaint that they then get victimised by that. So I think for that reason, if anyone decides to make a complaint they tend to go straight to [the integrity agency]…They tend to go outside because they feel that they might actually be a bit more protected than going internally.*
> **Manager**

Many of the legislative protections available to whistleblowers are predicated on the risks that can arise when information about wrongdoing becomes public—such as the threat of defamation action, or disciplinary or criminal action for breaching secrets.

Recognition of the importance of public whistleblowing—as a last resort or in exceptional circumstances—is an important principle of public interest disclosure legislation (Brown 2006:45; Brown et al. 2008a:261–8). Although most public employees currently report wrongdoing internally, it is in the public interest that employees are able to make public interest disclosures to journalists and Members of Parliament where no adequate reporting avenue exists, in any situation where it is simply not feasible for employees to report internally, or where existing reporting channels have failed to deal with issues effectively.

This principle is now recognised in legislation in a number of jurisdictions, including

- *Public Interest Disclosure Act 1998* (United Kingdom)
- *Public Interest Disclosure Act 1994* (NSW), s. 19
- *Public Interest Disclosure Act 2010* (Qld), s. 20
- by the Australian Government (2010; House of Representatives Standing Committee on Legal and Constitutional Affairs 2009).

Further, in 2011 the *Evidence Act* (Cwlth) was amended to exempt journalists from obligations to answer questions in court proceedings that would involve identifying their confidential sources.

In these jurisdictions, the fact that a public employee may legitimately take their disclosure public if it is not dealt with properly by agencies in the first instance provides a powerful incentive for agencies to take their whistleblowing responsibilities seriously.

Organisations have an obligation to advise their employees of their rights and obligations when it comes to reporting outside the organisation. All jurisdictions have confidentiality provisions that apply to public sector employees, as do most employment agreements with contractors. Organisations also have the task of encouraging employees to report wrongdoing but to do so realistically and to be clear on both practical and legal protections.

Even where legislative protection is yet to expressly extend to public whistleblowing, organisations should be wary of overemphasising confidentiality provisions, as rather than encouraging internal disclosures, this can discourage reporters from coming forward at all. It can be counterproductive to insist on enforcing confidentiality in circumstances where there is genuine public interest in disclosure.

PRACTICAL ACTION

Some approaches that organisations might find useful are

- multiple internal reporting pathways have implications for coordination and resourcing
- describing the role of organisations involved in external reporting pathways is necessary, but care will need to be taken not to make the explanation overly technical
- line managers need to be made aware that advising employees of external reporting pathways need not be threatening

- accentuating how the organisational culture welcomes transparency and external review is likely to have a positive influence on line managers so that when staff do exercise their rights to report externally, they do not suffer any adverse reaction

- both line managers and reporters need to be made aware that some external agencies who are the recipients of reports of wrongdoing are likely to refer the matter back to the organisation for action.

B4. ANONYMITY

Checklist item

- Clear advice that anonymous reports will be acted upon wherever possible, and about how anonymous reports/approaches may be made.

ANONYMOUS REPORTS

Organisations should accept anonymous reports, and give a commitment that they will be acted upon. Flexibility in reporting options will facilitate the reporting of wrongdoing. Assurances of anonymity might encourage risk-averse complainants to approach a disclosure point such as a hotline, even though most anonymous complainants do ultimately reveal their identity once they understand the likely investigation process and opportunities for confidentiality, discussed further in Section C3. Even though it is common to use the terms anonymity and confidentiality interchangeably, they are quite distinct concepts. The link between the two issues is clearly seen in Figure 3.1 in Section C3.

In some jurisdictions, organisations are required by legislation to receive anonymous and oral whistleblowing reports and in others protection is available only to those reporters who make a formal written report. While most agencies are flexible in terms of the form a report of wrongdoing may take, a significant proportion is not. When agencies (n = 304) were asked in Question 19 of the Agency Survey whether they would accept anonymous reports, while 68.1 per cent said 'yes', 28 per cent said 'no', with a 39 per cent non-response rate. Of those agencies that accepted anonymous reports, the estimated proportion of anonymous reports was 5.64 per cent.

Organisations are encouraged to note in their procedures that only those anonymous reports that contain enough information to support a proper response or investigation can support a commitment to take action. The recommended procedures below suggest how this issue might be addressed.

SAMPLE POLICIES AND PROCEDURES

Facilitating reporting

Who may report

These procedures apply to all staff of (name of organisation)

- permanent employees, whether full-time or part-time

- temporary or casual employees

- consultants

- contractors working for the organisation, including persons employed by the company or other organisation who has a contract with the public authority.

Note 1: In some jurisdictions, protection for reporters under the relevant legislation may extend beyond current employees to former employees or others.

What should be reported

Types of activities that may be reported

It is in the interests of (name of organisation) that staff report any kind of wrongdoing that they observe. This could include

- corrupt conduct
- fraud or theft
- official misconduct
- maladministration
- harassment or unlawful discrimination
- serious and substantial waste of public resources
- practices endangering the health or safety of the staff or community
- practices endangering the environment
- any other matter the reporter considers to be wrongdoing.

Note 2: The relevant public interest disclosure legislation may define activities that are protected, in which case, the list above might need to be adjusted. Organisations have the discretion to cite other matters beyond those described in the relevant legislation. If this is done, care should be taken to make it clear that any protection offered is internal organisational protection as distinct from that provided under the relevant public interest disclosure legislation.

Appropriate reporting points

Staff need to be advised of reporting processes for different categories of reports—for example, where and how to make reports about

- bullying and harassment
- public interest matters
- wrongdoing in another organisation
- reprisal action against a person who has reported wrongdoing
- occupational health and safety
- breaches of professional practice.

Level of information required

Potential reporters should be aware that they may be asked why they have come to the view that the activity or incident warrants reporting. Potential reporters do not need to demonstrate a legal level of proof, but should be prepared to demonstrate that they have reasonable grounds for their suspicions.

Reports may be made either in writing or verbally. Staff are encouraged to put the report in writing as soon as possible so that concerns can be communicated clearly in the reporter's own words. This will help to avoid any confusion or misinterpretation.

Should a disclosure be made verbally, this should be done in person through one of the internal reporting pathways described below. When this occurs, the recipient should make a comprehensive record of the report and provide it to the reporter to check, sign and date.

Where the reporter might be involved in wrongdoing

Reporting wrongdoing does not protect the reporter from any management, disciplinary or criminal action if the reporter has been involved in the wrongdoing or the reporter's performance is unsatisfactory. If, however, the reporter's involvement has been of a minor nature and the matter reported is serious, the organisation may choose not to take any action against the reporter because the reporter has brought forward the report.

The reporter is not protected if the reporter has deliberately provided false or misleading information.

Multiple reporting pathways

Internal reporting pathways

Staff wishing to report wrongdoing are encouraged to report the matter internally.

Potential reporters should consider who would be the best person to receive the report. If it is a matter that can be resolved by a line manager then the reporter should report it to them. Managers can be one of the best sources of support when reporting wrongdoing. If, however, it is a matter where the reporter is of the view that the line manager or senior people might be involved in the wrongdoing, the reporter should consider reporting it to the CEO or an external body.

(The following is a list of potential sources for the acceptance of reports of wrongdoing. These might need to be adjusted to take into account relevant legislative provisions or internal organisational policies.)

Reports of wrongdoing in the organisation may be made internally to

• a line manager

• any other person in a management position within the organisation

• the CEO (name, location and contact details provided)

• the Chair of the Audit Committee (name, location and contact details provided)

• specific officers designated to accept reports of wrongdoing; designated peer support officer or confidant (names, locations and contact details provided)

• specialist areas (such as an internal investigation unit or ethical standards unit— contact details will need to be included).

Note 3: It is recommended that the organisation formally nominate an officer in each work unit or location as a 'nominated whistleblowing officer' or some other more appropriate title. Also, it is recommended that, in medium to large organisations, a person is tasked with coordinating the whistleblower function. 'Whistleblower Report Coordinator' (or some other designation in accordance with organisational nomenclature) might be an appropriate title for such a function. Where such a position is designated, name, position title, location and contact details should be included in references to that position contained in the procedures.

External reporting pathways

Staff may choose to report wrongdoing to someone external to the organisation. This may be done as a first step, or if the reporter is not satisfied with the organisation's response to a report that was previously made.

While staff are urged to report to someone in the organisation, the organisation will respect and support a reporter in the event of a report to an appropriate external body.

(The following is a list of potential sources for the acceptance of reports of wrongdoing. These might need to be adjusted to take into account relevant legislative provisions or jurisdictional structure.)

- Anti-corruption body (Independent Commission Against Corruption, Crime and Misconduct Commission, Corruption and Crime Commission).
- Public Service/Merit Protection Commissioner.
- Auditor-General.
- Ombudsman.
- Police.

Reporters should be aware that when a report is made to an external body, it is very likely that the body will discuss their case with this organisation. This organisation will make every effort to assist and cooperate with that body to work towards a satisfactory outcome

Disclosure to the media

Reporters need to be aware that if they report matters to a person or an organisation that is not mentioned in these procedures, they will not be able to rely upon the protections afforded by the relevant legislation and may be in breach of the statutes dealing with the unauthorised release of information

Note 4: In New South Wales and Queensland, in limited circumstances, a report of wrongdoing may be made to a Member of Parliament or a journalist. Procedures in these jurisdictions need to provide precise advice of the conditions and limitations contained in the legislation.

Anonymity

The likelihood of a successful outcome is increased greatly if, when suspected wrongdoing is reported, the reporter makes their identity known. Nevertheless, reports of wrongdoing may be made anonymously, either in writing or by telephone. If a report is anonymous, the reporter will need to provide sufficient information for the matter to be investigated, as it will not be possible to go back to the reporter for clarification or more detail.

Provided enough detail has been provided, the organisation is committed to acting upon the report.

Reporters should note that in the event an anonymous report is made

- it will not be possible for the organisation to keep the reporter informed of the progress in handling the report
- the reporter could experience difficulties in relying upon the protections afforded by the relevant legislation
- the support mechanisms normally available to reporters will not be available
- an anonymous report is no guarantee that another employee might not identify the reporter as the source of the report.

Whether or not a report has been made anonymously, the fewer people who know about the disclosure—both before and after it has been made—the more likely it is that the organisation will be able to protect the reporter from any detrimental action in reprisal. Potential (or actual) reporters should be encouraged not to talk about the matter to work colleagues or any other unauthorised person.

C.

ASSESSMENT AND INVESTIGATION OF REPORTS

I think people are quite confused about what can be dealt with at what level. I was certainly confused about my role when minor complaints are allocated down to me as to exactly what was expected of me with that complaint—was it my job to resolve it, was it my job to investigate it but put it back to [the central investigating unit] to be resolved, what's an achievable resolution, if I've got word against word how is that to work, what does 'substantiated' mean?
Manager

Competent investigation of whistleblowing reports followed by an effective response is a key objective of any whistleblowing program. Responses rely on effective assessment of what the disclosure is about, so that it can be handled in the most appropriate way. Several key elements are needed to ensure these processes are in place. These include comprehensive agency systems for recording and tracking employee reports of wrongdoing and improved basic training for public sector managers on how to recognise and respond to possible public interest disclosures (Brown and Wheeler 2008:304–6). There is also a need to preserve and manage confidentiality, to begin planning for when confidentiality is not available, and to deal with issues of equity and natural justice that often arise at early stages of investigations.

A startling 97 per cent of public interest whistleblowing occurs internally in agencies, with the bulk of this occurring to supervisors and line managers, rather than to reporting hotlines or internal specialists in the first instance (Donkin et al. 2008:90). An overwhelming majority of reports of wrongdoing might not end up being handled within the formal reporting processes of the organisation, due to the common ambiguity about when reports should be handled informally by line managers and when they should be dealt with by formal reporting processes.

The very positive finding about reporters' preference for internal reporting places a number of obligations upon organisations and line managers. It would be beneficial to develop and promulgate policies that clearly set out

• when managers should handle matters themselves

• whether and where reports should be recorded

• when reports should be referred to internal or external organisational mechanisms.

Efforts to support and protect employees who report wrongdoing ideally should commence at the point of disclosure, rather than when problems begin to arise. Risk-management processes, in particular, could be built into the early stages of the assessment and investigation of disclosures.

C1. IDENTIFICATION AND TRACKING OF REPORTS

Checklist items

‒ A coordinated system for tracking all significant reports of wrongdoing (including grievances) at all levels of the organisation, including clear advice to supervisors on when, how and whom to notify about staff complaints and possible whistleblowing reports.

‒ Organisational procedure for mandatory reporting to regulatory or integrity agencies on whistleblowing reports, including early notification of significant or higher-risk reports.

TRACKING REPORTS OF WRONGDOING

Most agencies currently lack sufficiently comprehensive systems for recording and tracking employee reports of wrongdoing. Systems for recording and tracking reports of wrongdoing are a basic prerequisite to effective monitoring of how many public interest disclosures are being made, what investigation or other action is being taken, and how those involved in the disclosures are being managed, at both an agency and a whole-of-government level. They enable senior management of agencies to know what disclosures are being received at junior and middle management levels. This is where the bulk of disclosures are currently received, and where the key risks of mismanagement, mistreatment or reprisal arise. Based upon discussions in workshops of industry partners and representatives of case-study agencies, it is suggested organisations need to put into place integrated systems to mitigate the risk of mismanagement of disclosures, particularly to

- allow senior management to track reports and report-related issues wherever they are being dealt with throughout the organisation, including informally by lower level managers

- record and track wrongdoing reports in a coordinated way, together with other forms of complaints, grievances and conflicts

- record and track all reports that might possibly be classified as public interest disclosures (PIDs) under legislation

- require all reports to be assessed at the outset for the level of reprisal risk or other conflict associated with the making of the report, classified according to risk and routinely monitored for any change in risk level (see Section C2).

UNDER THE RADAR? ADVICE TO MANAGERS ON FORMAL AND INFORMAL HANDLING

There appears to be a large discrepancy between the number of cases that organisations reported as being handled and the number of reports of wrongdoing indicated by surveyed employees (Brown et al. 2008b:44, Table 2.12). One explanation for the discrepancy is that many of the reports made by employees were done so informally to line managers and other supervisors. There was near unanimity among the managers and case-handlers that informal reporting occurred in their organisations. In interviews with managers and case-handlers, some ventured an opinion on the proportion of reports that were informal, with estimates of informal reports ranging from 10 per cent to 98 per cent. The huge differences in estimates indicate that managers were not aware of what was occurring in the organisation outside their immediate work group.

The advantages of dealing with reports of wrongdoing informally include

- matters can be handled quickly

- potential problems can be 'nipped in the bud'

- the administrative burden of the formal reporting process can be avoided

- reporters do not feel intimidated by the legality and adversarial nature of the formal reporting process

- there is capacity to prevent issues becoming formal unnecessarily—for example, if there is a clear lack of merit in the report or personality difference only

- it enables a graduated response that gives reporters the opportunity to consider options as to how they would prefer the report to be handled

- line managers are able to deal with improper behaviour immediately and give wrongdoers a 'gentle nudge' to get them back on the right track so the workplace can move on. This enables managers to deal with 'rash behaviour' that might be best kept out of formal reporting systems.

Managers perceived handling matters informally as an important part of their day-to-day managerial responsibilities. When a problem is elevated to a formal report, often the line managers are concerned about negative perceptions about

> *I think people are quite confused about what can be dealt with at what level. I was certainly confused about my role when minor complaints are allocated down to me as to exactly what was expected of me with that complaint—was it my job to resolve it, was it my job to investigate it but put it back to [the central investigating unit] to be resolved, what's an achievable resolution, if I've got word against word how is that to work, what does 'substantiated' mean?*
> **Manager**

managerial ability. Informal reporting can also be viewed as a self-protection mechanism in that, as one manager observed, it 'can't come back to bite you later in your career'.

The disadvantages of informal reporting can include

- reports are often swept 'under the mat' rather than the problem being examined

- the perception could arise in the workplace that nothing has been done, leading to mistrust in the workplace and serious issues being left unresolved

- there can be a subjective dimension to informal reporting when a particular manager does not trust the bona fides of the reporter and will handle the matter formally, for the manager's own protection

- a corollary of this approach is when a manager has a positive relationship with the reporter or the subject of the allegations, and this distorts their neutrality—or the perception of their neutrality—in handling the case informally

- handling reports informally also makes it difficult to consistently articulate the expectations of the organisation

- some managers might not take informal reports seriously and might attempt to mediate a situation, even when there is a significant underlying problem and systemic change is required.

In addition, informal reporting is a mechanism that facilitates the covering up of wrongdoing or inappropriate behaviour. Informal reporting often hides missing patterns of behaviour that could indicate endemic problems within the organisation. Whether or not these are serious public interest or personnel matters, the organisation ideally should know about them so as to take effective and coordinated action.

Given that managers recognise the problems with informal reporting, it is not surprising that some organisations have designed solutions for dealing with them. Organisations such as police forces often have to be a lot more meticulous in their handling of reports of wrongdoing. Figure 2.1 in the previous section described the inaction rates of employees in the case-study agencies. Some police services were among those organisations surveyed and, while their inaction rates were lower than other agencies in the sample, they were still of an order that suggests that even implementing compulsory reporting systems with universal coverage does not ensure employees will report all wrongdoing that they have witnessed. One solution is to have a policy of recording and assessing every complaint or report of possible wrongdoing, but still leaving line managers to deal with the majority of reports.

While that approach resolves the issue of recording matters, it does not, however, necessarily address the informal reporting problems outlined above. Even in those organisations where there was a highly formalised and elaborate system of reporting, interviews with managers and case-handlers indicated that confusion about staff obligations and what should be reported still existed. In addition to implementing policy for the recording of wrongdoing, it is also necessary for organisations to educate employees on what needs to be reported, what does not need to be reported and the processes for so doing.

It is also desirable for organisations to set criteria that would enable a coherent and logical practice for filtering those reports that can be handled appropriately in the immediate workplace from those that will need to be dealt with more formally. Most managers nominated the seriousness of the wrongdoing as being the key consideration. Other criteria nominated were the number of people who were affected by the activity being reported and the potential impact upon morale of the work unit. Similar to the need to record all reports, however, nominating criteria to distinguish informal from formal reports appeared to be more of an aspiration than a reality in most organisations.

Given the number of reports that line managers handle on a day-to-day basis and the sheer complexity of many public sector organisations, it is a major challenge for any organisation to have a clearly articulated set of streaming criteria that can be applied consistently across the organisation.

The response to this issue arguably needs more than the promulgation of sophisticated and comprehensive procedures for the reporting and handling of wrongdoing. In a perfect organisation, all potential recipients of reports of wrongdoing would be clear in their own minds what sorts of issues they can deal with themselves and what sorts of issues need to be formally notified or referred to others in or outside the organisation. Where that line is drawn might not directly correspond with the distinction between employment-related grievances and public interest wrongdoing (discussed in Section C2). Some disclosure-related grievances (such as systemic sexual harassment) are of such seriousness that the response calls for coordination from a higher level than first-level managers.

Achieving a state where line managers are quite clear about their reporting obligations is not merely an issue of the transmission of skills. It is an issue of organisational culture. What is being suggested here is embarking upon a program of clarifying when line managers have the independence and autonomy to handle reports and when the organisation should take coordinated action to deal with the wrongdoing reported and notify external agencies.

EARLY NOTIFICATION TO EXTERNAL AGENCIES

Ideally, agency systems for recording and tracking disclosures should extend to automatic systems for early notification of external regulatory or integrity agencies about significant or higher-risk reports. As a disclosure is logged and assessed, there could be routine notification of external agencies of matters triggering mandatory reporting requirements, other serious matters, any high-risk matters, and all alleged reprisals or cases of detrimental action.

Such a procedure recognises that there are many circumstances where an agency is better placed in knowing that another appropriate agency such as the police, an anti-corruption body or the lead agency in their jurisdiction for public interest disclosures is aware of the matter and able to intervene to provide advice or assistance with its resolution, if required. This is a recommendation made in the first report (Brown et al. 2008a:285) and requires government decision. Logically, it follows that such a notification system requires that at least one coordinating integrity agency have the statutory authority and capacity to track whistleblowing cases, and maintain an effective supportive monitoring and oversight role, including the ability to respond to early requests for assistance where need arises.

PRACTICAL ACTION

The characteristics of a good reporting system within a public sector organisation are that it would

- have a low threshold for reporting so that senior management can track reports regardless of whether they are being dealt with formally or informally, and early intervention to protect reporters could be taken

- be a part of an integrated reporting system that includes grievances and the reporting of other sorts of incidents, complaints or conflicts
- require assessment and monitoring of all reports for the risk of reprisal or related conflict
- include *prime facie* minor incidents that could indicate patterns of more serious behaviour
- clearly define the separate roles and responsibilities of the decentralised points of authority and the central coordinating area.

C2. ASSESSMENT PROCEDURES

Checklist items

- Management procedures and skills for differentiating, as appropriate, between different types of wrongdoing (including grievances), and initiating appropriate action.
- A flexible approach to the types, level and formality of investigations to be conducted, including clear criteria for when no further action is required.
- Early and continuing assessment of the risks of reprisal, workplace conflict or other adverse outcomes involving whistleblowers or other witnesses.

DIFFERENTIATING BETWEEN TYPES OF WRONGDOING

The issue of differentiation between personal grievances and public interest disclosures is more complex than it would first appear. The orthodox position is that there is a duality of disclosures, with separate reporting points for complaints dealing with personnel issues and complaints with a public interest component, and different specialist units that are responsible for ensuring appropriate action is taken in response. Public interest disclosure legislation reinforces this orthodoxy by validating the distinction in legislation, which is then often reinforced in organisational procedures.

Interviews with reporters' managers and case-handlers indicated the reality is more complex. In practice, reporters of wrongdoing do not make this distinction between grievances and public interest matters, and the types of complaints made lie across the spectrum.

Managers and case-handlers had different perspectives about this issue. Some accepted the orthodox position and saw a clear distinction. As one manager said: 'If it's just a personal conflict and there is no unethical or improper behaviour whatsoever…[it] needs to be dealt with just as HR [human resources].' Another group of managers and case-handlers recognised that in practice there is ambiguity and accepted that some issues, such as bullying, did not neatly fit within the two categories. One investigator noted that some grievances were so serious 'that they went well beyond the relationship dimensions'.

To gain further insight into the complexity of the relationship between grievances and matters of public interest, the surveys asked reporters to identify issues that were occurring at the same time as they were making a report of wrongdoing, and asked managers and case-handlers what they thought the main issues were for reporters. Table 3.1 sets out the self-assessment of case-study agency whistleblowers and the estimates of case-handlers and managers about the prevalence of such mixed reports. Reporters were asked to nominate whether a series of circumstances related to pre-existing management or personnel difficulties coexisted with their decision to report. Managers and case-handlers were asked whether they thought those same sets of issues were related to the report. In other words, reporters were asked a factual question and managers/case-handlers were asked to attribute motivation to the reporters.

TABLE 3.1

Comparison of internal witness circumstances coexistent with making a report with managers' and case-handlers' attribution

Issue	Internal witnesses (n = 214)		Managers (n = 860)	
	Issues cited (%)	Ranking of issues	Mean	Ranking of issues
Conflict or serious disagreement with the employee's manager(s) or supervisor(s)	37.1	1	3.22	1
Dissatisfaction with one or more agency policies	12.6	2	2.88	7
Dissatisfaction with the employee's work duties	11.7	3	2.97	4
Another grievance against the employee's manager(s) or supervisor(s)	11.6	4	3.01	3
A decision about a promotion that affected the employee	11.2	5	2.73	6
Conflict or serious disagreement with the employee's co-worker(s)	10.7	6	3.22	1
Another grievance against the employee's co-workers	4.9	7	2.95	5
Failure to renew the employee's contract	0.5	8	2.04	8

Notes: Internal witnesses (n = 224) were asked: 'When you first reported or provided information about the wrongdoing, were any of the following already causing you concern?' Respondents were able to circle more than one option. Managers and case-handlers (n = 860) were asked: 'When employees first report wrongdoing, how often do you think any of the following issues were already also causing them concern?' (1 = never, 2 = rarely, 3 = sometimes, 4 = often, 5 = always, 6 = don't know). The list of issues was identical.

Sources: Question 23 of the Internal Witness Survey and Question 26 of the Case-Handler and Manager Survey.

The results above indicated that there was a divergence of perspectives between reporters and managers/case-handlers. The following is a summary.

- Both groups agreed that conflict or serious disagreement with supervisors was the most common existing situation at the time of reporting—cited by 37.1 per cent of reporters. That issue was also rated highly by managers and case-handlers, but was ranked equally highest with another issue: conflict or serious disagreement with the employee's co-workers. While managers and case-handlers saw the issue as being important, its importance was *underestimated*.

- Managers and case-handlers also *underestimated* the importance of reporters' dissatisfaction with agency policies.

- Managers and case-handlers *overestimated* the importance of reporters' conflict or serious disagreement with co-workers.

- Managers and case-handlers appeared to agree with reporters on the importance of
    - decisions about promotion

   Roberts | Brown | Olsen

from participating agencies. Similarly, when asked if anyone in the organisation had responsibility for ensuring risk assessments were conducted when a report of wrongdoing was received, the 'no response' rate of agencies was very high. Very few organisations were found to have formal risk-management procedures that could be applied to reporters.

There is a disturbing lack of interest in agencies in establishing procedures to assess risk and implementing structures to ensure that risk assessments actually take place. During interviews, managers and investigators were probed about the use of risk-management techniques in the area of whistleblowing. Almost universally, respondents indicated that risk management was rarely applied to the whistleblowing process and, if it was, it was not usually done very well. One manager described it as an 'afterthought'. This was one of the major shortcomings identified in the assessment of procedures and practices for dealing with employees who report wrongdoing (Roberts 2008:246, Table 10.8).

Undertaking some level of risk management upon receipt of a report implies that recipients have some level of skill and comprehension in the procedure. When asked about what training officers authorised to receive reports were provided with (n = 297, Question 15 of the Agency Survey), agencies reported that 43.1 per cent had no training, 49.8 per cent had only informal training and 22.9 per cent were professionally trained. Given that 97 per cent of initial reports were made internally, and most of these to line managers, it is clear that considerable variation exists in the levels of preparation and training being given to recipients of the initial reports.

While risk management is primarily employed to determine the risk of reprisal against a reporter, the workshops of industry partners and representatives of case-study agencies highlighted that the process can, and should, be utilised to assess and treat all the risks related to the reporting of wrongdoing. Risks additional to reprisal include

- risk of damage to the reputation of a third party if allegations of wrongdoing have been made against another employee of the organisation

- risk of paralysing the reporter's work unit if the issue is not managed optimally

- risk that the reporter might breach confidentiality requirements and speak to the media before the organisation has had the opportunity to deal with the issue

- risk of adverse health effects to the reporter, the subject officer or any other person affected by the making of the report.

PRACTICAL ACTION

The internal procedures of public sector organisations should be capable of initiating appropriate action or investigation that is relevant to the report received. Most organisations have established processes for dealing with workplace grievances, and can simply stream these matters into that process. Appropriate action needs to be taken, however, in response to public interest disclosures, including by way of investigation either by internal or by external resources. The shortcomings outlined above could be addressed by managers being provided with guidance on how matters should be streamed and dealt with in both organisational procedures and relevant training.

As noted above, the current standard of investigations conducted by public sector organisations is perceived as low. Based upon interviews with managers and case-handlers, organisations can improve investigations at the administrative level by

- resourcing the investigation function adequately

- ensuring robust administrative structures, including clear accountability structures for those staff tasked with investigations and comprehensive investigation guidelines

- selecting staff with expertise in investigations or ensuring adequate training is undertaken (where organisations do not have in-house investigation resources, they will need to provide managers with practical guidance on undertaking an investigation); the following references are two generic investigation guides (Crime and Misconduct Commission 2007; ICAC 2009)

- where necessary, using investigation staff from outside the immediate work area where the report has been made

- providing auditors with greater powers to investigate

- freeing staff undertaking investigations from their regular duties

- if not already in place, establishing a whole-of-agency investigation unit

- employing senior investigators at appropriate pay rates to avoid the problems associated with junior staff investigating more senior staff

- ensuring external investigators are available for serious and controversial issues.

At a procedural level, organisations can improve the standard of their investigations by

- ensuring timeliness in investigation outcomes

- undertaking investigations in accordance with professional standards

- following up reports of wrongdoing by taking statements or seeking further information from reporters

- communicating more effectively with external providers

- ensuring good investigation processes and procedures are in place

- having review, planning and mentoring processes in place

- committing to providing natural justice to all parties

- exploring informal resolution processes, particularly mediation or other management action.

Finally, organisations tend to place a low emphasis upon the issue of dealing with reprisals against and other adverse outcomes for reporters. All solutions to this problem begin with early and ongoing identification of risk, and the implementation of prevention or containment strategies that are aligned accordingly.

Appendix II of this guide contains a practical introduction to undertaking a risk assessment based on lessons from the research. Performing a risk assessment of the likelihood of reprisals and adverse outcomes can be a quite difficult task. In particular, the persons assessing risk need to clearly define the individual factors of the reporter (both organisational and personal) that could influence the process or the chances of risks materialising.

Checklist items

- Commitment to the confidentiality of whistleblowing reports to the maximum extent possible, including

  - procedures for maintaining the confidentiality of whistleblowers, persons against whom allegations have been made, and other witnesses to the maximum extent possible

  - clear advice about possible limits of confidentiality

  - procedures for consulting and, wherever possible, gaining consent of whistleblowers prior to any action that could identify them, including to external agencies.

- Procedures for determining when confidentiality cannot be ensured, and active strategies for supporting employees and managing workplaces where confidentiality is not possible or cannot be maintained.

THE IMPORTANCE OF CONFIDENTIALITY

The issue of confidentiality is closely linked to anonymity, which was discussed in Section B4. That link is clearly seen in Figure 3.1.

Protecting the confidentiality of a reporter of wrongdoing is often perceived as important, and organisations are perceived as effective when they have such measures in place. Maintaining confidentiality is important from the perspective of case-handlers and reporters. In the Case-Handler and Manager Survey, case-handlers (n = 253) and managers (n = 394) were asked: 'What are the most important things that could be changed within your organisation to ensure that wrongdoing in your organisation is reported more often and dealt with more effectively?' Issues relating to confidentiality were mentioned by 16 case-handlers and 23 managers.

In interviews, many managers and case-handlers indicated a desire for confidentiality in the handling of reports of wrongdoing; they considered it important for protecting reporters; they believed it required greater emphasis; and yet many saw the confidentiality processes within their organisations as being less than optimal. They were pessimistic about the possibility of protecting reporters' confidentiality. In practice, it might be impossible to keep the identity of a reporter confidential for a number of reasons.

> *There are certain difficulties [with confidentiality]. One of the things I do tell people straight up is that we will protect their confidentiality as much as we can, but as you know, it may come to a point where we can't progress the complaint unless maybe they will be identified. We spend a lot of time with people to make sure they're comfortable to go on with the investigation. Often I think it's the case that people tend to leave [the organisation] and [then] make a complaint.*
> **Manager**

- Many managers see a conflict between maintaining confidentiality and the principles of natural justice. When a report of wrongdoing involves allegations against another staff member, even though, technically, there is no requirement to reveal the identity of the reporter, this was frequently deduced, particularly in small workgroups.

- Strict application of confidentiality processes can limit the capacity of an organisation to provide support for a reporter. Some reporters indicated that because of the confidentiality provisions, they were constrained from talking to their colleagues about the report and therefore could not avail themselves of their support.

- There can be overriding legal obligations that conflict with protecting the confidentiality of a reporter.

- Reporters might inadvertently reveal their identity or the report might be part of a sequence of events initiated overtly by the reporter. In many cases, by the time someone is approaching their organisation to make a report, they will have already discussed the issue with others.

• When action is taken by management to deal with a report of wrongdoing, work colleagues will often attempt to guess the identity of the reporter—sometimes getting it right and sometimes getting it wrong.

• Some reporters indicated in the interviews that they believed that management had breached their confidentiality; however, that attitude appeared to be based upon expectations of confidentiality that might have been unrealistic.

Strict adherence to the principles of confidentiality can impede the progress of an investigation. This can occur when a report is made to an integrity agency and then that integrity agency refers the matter back to the organisation, without revealing the identity of the reporter, or if the identity of the reporter is known internally only by the internal witness support unit. In these cases, investigators might have difficulty in successfully investigating the case because they cannot interview or seek further information from the reporter.

Finally, confidentiality did not emerge as a risk factor of whistleblower mistreatment (Brown and Olsen 2008b:149). This is probably because, while confidentiality is important for as long as it can be preserved, in many cases, it is simply not an option or ceases to be an option.

FIGURE 3.1

Anonymous and confidential approach flow chart

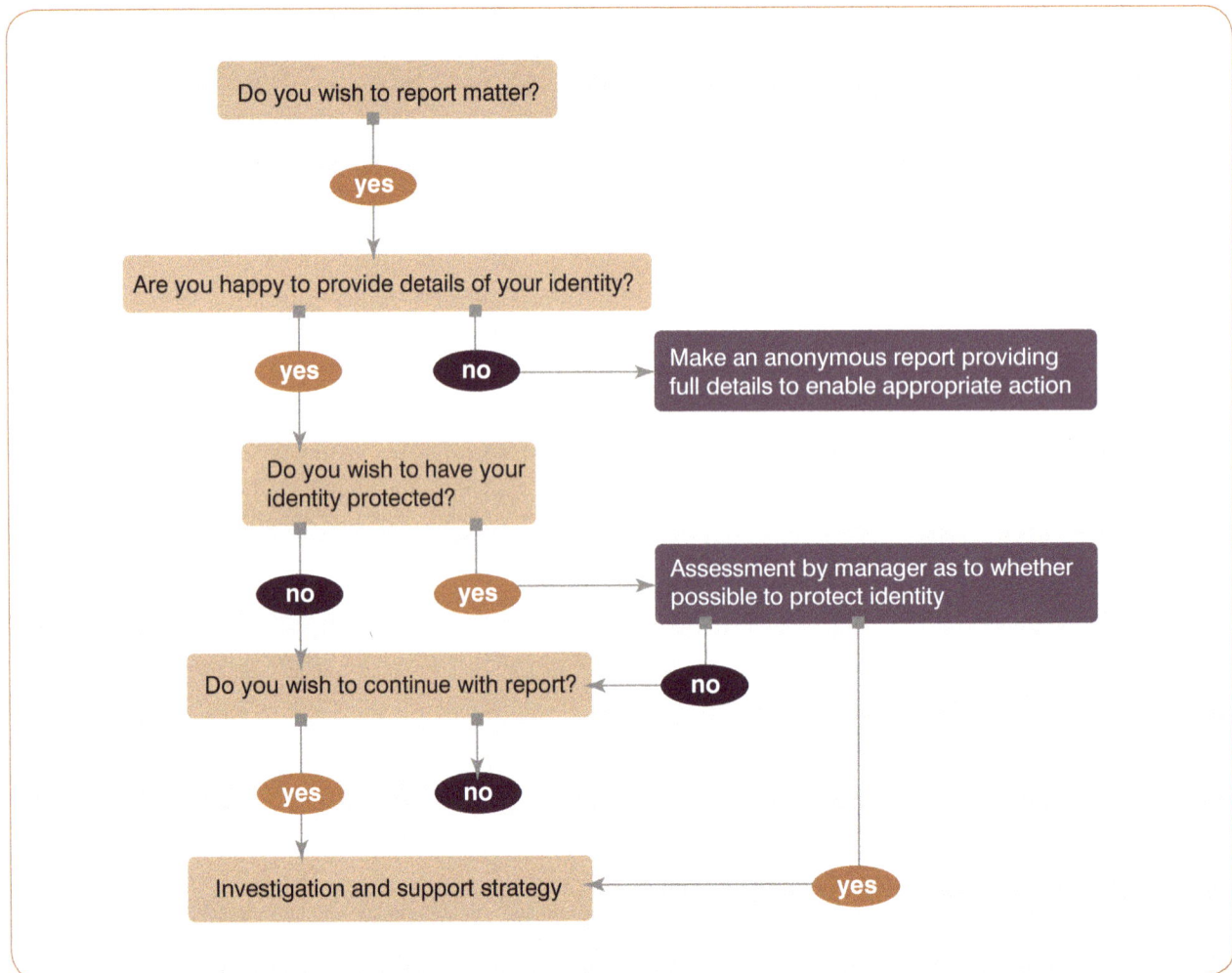

CONSULTING ON CONFIDENTIALITY DECISIONS

In circumstances where confidentiality cannot be maintained or it is desirable for the whistleblower's identity to be revealed to any person, it is vital that the whistleblower is consulted and, if possible, their informed consent obtained for the decision regarding the desirable action. In some circumstances, the optimal way of dealing with the issues raised by the report might be to explain to all the staff concerned what has happened and what has been done, and publicly commending the whistleblower for bringing the matter forward. Such a strategy should, however, be undertaken only in appropriate circumstances with the fully informed consent of the whistleblower and if they have appropriate support.

WHEN CONFIDENTIALITY CEASES OR IS IMPOSSIBLE

The practical difficulties in maintaining confidentiality raise a complex dilemma for the organisation and, in particular, the recipient of the report. Reporters might fear reprisals, and assurances about (and expectations of) confidentiality can maintain the reporter's confidence in the process. The recipient of the report, however, also faces an obligation to honestly advise the staff member about the possibility of confidentiality not being maintained. This could dissuade the reporter from providing further information about the wrongdoing and thus the organisation might lose the opportunity to investigate and correct a potentially serious problem.

There is also a chronological dimension to maintaining confidentiality, as confidentiality can be easier to safeguard at the beginning of the reporting process. As more people within the organisation, or even externally, come to know about the report, confidentiality becomes more difficult to maintain. While this is the reality of dealing with whistleblower reports, it might not be any comfort to the reporter. When an organisation receives a report, there is a relatively short time frame within which an investigation can be launched unimpeded by issues of compromised confidentiality.

Misunderstandings around the requirements of natural justice are a source of confusion and practical difficulty in the area of maintaining confidentiality. When an allegation is made against a person, natural justice principles require that the person be made aware of the allegations against them if an adverse decision is to be made. Many managers, however, incorrectly assume that natural justice obligations require the identity of the person making the report to be revealed. In small work groups, making someone aware of the allegations against them can also inevitably mean signalling the identity of the reporter.

PRACTICAL ACTION

Being realistic. Assurances given to the reporter about confidentiality need to be realistic, but not couched in terms that will stop them from proceeding. This is not simply a matter of establishing procedures for routinely explaining the likely outcomes to potential reporters. Rather, it involves creating an environment and a culture whereby all employees (and potential reporters) have confidence that they will be treated well by managers and by co-workers for reporting wrongdoing. It is important that potential whistleblowers are given credible commitments regarding confidentiality as well as accurate advice regarding the circumstances in which confidentiality might not be able to be maintained.

Dealing with the issue early. Ideally, organisations should use the window of opportunity for confidentiality at the start of the process to identify strategies for supporting the reporter while confidentiality still acts as a temporary shield. Without detracting from the requirements of legislation, organisations need to be realistic about their capacity to safeguard confidentiality and should take a proactive approach to managing the (usually inevitable) disclosure of the reporter's identity.

Consultation. In circumstances where confidentiality cannot be maintained or it is desirable for the whistleblower's identity to be revealed to any person, it is most desirable that the whistleblower be consulted and, if possible, their informed consent is obtained. In some situations, the optimal way of dealing with the issues raised by the report might be to explain to all staff concerned what has happened and what has been done, and publicly commend the whistleblower for bringing the matter forward. Such a strategy should, however, be undertaken only in circumstances where the whistleblower has the necessary support and with the fully informed consent of the whistleblower.

Awareness. It is suggested that training for line managers include practical advice on the meaning of natural justice. Where possible, there should be readily accessible advice to line managers on how to handle the competing pressures of confidentiality and affording natural justice.

Confidentiality checklist. Practical considerations for line managers, specialist internal units or external watchdog agencies responding to issues of confidentiality include

- who knows about the report
- is the organisation required to notify an external agency that the disclosure has been received
- has the reporter told anybody that they reported or were thinking about reporting
- is it obvious from the nature of the disclosure who has made it
- what is the risk to the reporter or their colleagues if their identity is revealed
- what is the risk to the investigation if the organisation reveals any information that suggests the identity of the reporter at this point?

It is suggested that in dealing with the issue of confidentiality, a key principle is that confidentiality is highly desirable but subject to practical limitations. In procedures and in training, a difficult balance needs to be struck between encouraging reporters to come forward and not raising expectations of confidentiality that are unable to be realised.

> *I think we do our best to support bona fide reporters and that's why I've always argued with senior management that we can't go after people who've been vexatious. Because, even though you'd really like to sometimes, because you see what fallout their horrid behaviour has done to some people, you cannot risk frightening genuine complainants off. Complainants tell you a whole lot of useful things about your services and how you deliver your services. And there are a lot of very vulnerable people out there who have great difficulty making a complaint. It's not that there is this sea of nasty people out there wanting to make complaints*
> **Manager**

C4. EQUITY AND NATURAL JUSTICE

Checklist items

- Clear procedures for the protection of the rights of persons against whom allegations have been made, including appropriate sanctions against
    - false or vexatious allegations
    - unreasonable breaches of confidentiality.
- Clear advice to managers about to whom, when and by whom information about allegations of wrongdoing need to be given, for reasons such as natural justice.

In formal whistleblowing policies and their implementation, a number of organisations recognised the need to treat staff at all levels within the organisation equitably (Roberts 2008:246, Table 10.8). This means that all members of the organisation who make disclosures, or have disclosures made about them, are dealt with fairly and consistently.

The issue of confidentiality for those against whom allegations had been made was considered to be important by participants in the study, as outlined in Table 3.2.

TABLE 3.2

Managers' and case-handlers' views on the importance of protecting confidentiality for those against whom allegations had been made

Statement	Case-handlers (n = 338)		Managers (n = 534)	
	Mean	SD	**Mean**	SD
Importance of protecting the identity of the subject of allegations (1 = not at all to 5 = extremely)	**4.39**	0.71	**4.38**	0.68

Source: Question 57 of the Case-Handler and Manager Survey.

Manager *(when asked about the impact of a report of wrongdoing upon the person against whom the allegation was made):*

Just totally devastated by the fact that someone makes an accusation and their integrity has been questioned even though the person has come back with the evidence and said that it is not correct. There is no right of reply. The [name of the investigation entity] inquiry can destroy a person's self-belief, their belief in their own worth, their value to the organisation.

The issue of whether persons against whom allegations have been made received the same level of support as was afforded to whistleblowers prompted some passionate responses. The issue of protection of the subject of allegations was raised in 16 of the 34 interviews: six interviewees believed that the subject of allegations needed support; two indicated that they thought that reporters needed more support than the subject of allegations; and five interviewees indicated that there should be a balance and that both parties to the dispute needed support. It is clear that many managers felt that the processes of support and protection for reporters were weighted unfairly against the persons about whom allegations have been made. The interviews also highlighted that, where reports of wrongdoing involving managers are made, those managers' colleagues can be placed in a difficult situation.

Such attitudes are not typical, however, of the response of managers and case-handlers to this question. The overwhelming majority of respondents expressed support for a balanced and even-handed treatment of both sides in this often-adversarial situation.

Section A discussed the attitudes of managers when a report of wrongdoing was an allegation against another staff member. These sorts of reports are not infrequent and create significant difficulties for organisations. As mentioned in that section, this is a cultural issue where, ideally, managers are aware that the rights and interests of all parties need to be protected. The sample procedures below contain suggestions as to how this might be achieved.

APPROPRIATE SANCTIONS AGAINST FALSE OR VEXATIOUS ALLEGATIONS

When reports of wrongdoing are made, they frequently involve specific allegations against a particular individual. This has the effect of creating an adversarial situation and, unless it is handled in a transparent and even-handed way, enables those within the organisation who are sceptical about the value of whistleblowing to claim that it has a corrosive effect by encouraging unfounded allegations that can damage professional reputations.

This is another emotion-charged area of whistleblowing and can cause considerable concerns within organisations. In reality, the problem of false or vexatious disclosures appears to be overstated and most managers have a more balanced view of disclosures. Of the 34 interviews with managers and case-handlers, only five mentioned malicious or vexatious reporters.

Nevertheless, it is likely that line managers might feel under threat from the risk of false or vexatious allegations, and this can be addressed only by ensuring thorough, transparent and even-handed investigation processes. Relatively few organisations included any description of sanctions for those making false or vexatious allegations in their whistleblowing procedures: of the 24 items assessed in the analysis of agency procedures, sanctions for those making false or vexatious allegations were ranked twenty-first (Roberts 2008:246, Table 10.8). Organisations are encouraged to include this element in their procedures and also to include in their awareness-rating programs that the organisation will be neutral and even-handed in investigating and dealing with reporter complaints that involve a particular employee.

> [C]omplainants use the protected disclosure legislation really badly and use it for their own interests and make vexatious complaints against their colleagues and their managers, etc. And because everyone is so damned terrified to actually deal with those sorts of vexatious matters—for the fear of being seen to be doing detrimental action—people get away with absolute murder in terms of the level of complaints they make about their colleagues. **Manager**

NATURAL JUSTICE

It is a common misconception that confidentiality is often breached because it is a requirement of natural justice. In interviews, many managers and investigators insisted that it was necessary for the name of a reporter to be revealed when a serious allegation was made against another person. The quotation in the box encapsulates this belief.

Natural justice typically does not require the revelation of a reporter's name. Natural justice requires that the person against whom the allegation is made is told of the substance of the allegation and given the opportunity to refute it, *prior to any decision regarding action being taken against them*.

> I'm no expert, but I do understand the legislation and its intent…My understanding is that, in certain circumstances, you do have to make the complainant's name available because it may be the only way that you can actually put fairly serious allegations to someone. **Manager**

PRACTICAL ACTION

Reports of wrongdoing that allege wrongdoing by another employee are not infrequent and create significant difficulties for organisations. Ideally, the ethical culture of an organisation would promote fair treatment and support for all parties involved in a report, and managers would be fully aware of how to protect the rights and interests of all parties. The sample procedures below contain suggestions as to how this might be achieved.

Organisations are encouraged to include sanctions for those making false or vexatious allegations in their procedures. Additionally, awareness-raising programs should promote the organisation's commitment to dealing with and investigating reports that involve employees in an objective and transparent manner.

In some jurisdictions, there is a legislative requirement that organisations may only provide the name of the reporter for natural justice purposes if it is unlikely that a reprisal will be taken against them as a result of that disclosure and it is essential to do so for the purposes of natural justice. That approach clearly has some benefits, and organisations are encouraged to consider including this in their own procedures.

While the subject of the allegations might come to their own conclusion as to the identity of the reporter, it is not a requirement for organisations to reveal this information. It is suggested that organisations provide clear advice to supervisors and managers about to whom, when and by whom information about allegations needs to be given to persons affected by a report of wrongdoing, for reasons such as natural justice.

SAMPLE POLICIES AND PROCEDURES

Assessment and investigation of reports

Identification and tracking of reports

In addition to the issues listed in 'Practical Action' in Section C1 and subject to the consideration below, all reports of wrongdoing will be recorded and notified to the 'Whistleblower Report Coordinator' mentioned in the 'Sample policies and procedures: Section C' (name, position title, location and contact details). That notification will include

- identification number of report
- name of reporter (where reporter has consented)
- recipient of the report
- date and time
- nature of the allegation; if the report has been made in writing, this should be attached
- relation to other reports (if known)
- to whom the report has been referred for investigation.

At each step in the handling of the report, the responsible officer shall notify the officer listed above of

- results of preliminary assessment of the risk of reprisal
- an active process of checking with relevant line managers of any suspicions that reprisals might be occurring
- if no further action is to be taken on the report, reasons for that decision
- feedback provided to the reporter at each stage in the process
- details of support offered and provided
- if an investigation occurs, name of investigating officer and the outcomes
- referral or notification to external integrity agency or agencies
- contact with the subject of the allegation
- any remedial action taken as a result of the report
- reasons and process for ceasing support for the reporter.

Assessment procedures

The responsibilities of the officer receiving the report are to

- maintain the confidentiality of the reporter and any person who is the subject of allegations
- address whether the report requires further investigation to establish the facts and to advise the Whistleblower Report Coordinator of the outcome of that consideration
- advise the reporter not to discuss the report with anyone else
- explain to the reporter what will happen as a result of the report
- if requested, make arrangements to meet the reporter discreetly
- advise the reporter of the desirability of putting the report in writing
- advise the reporter of the organisational support mechanisms available and the names and contact details of that support as well as any relevant organisational function (such as the Whistleblower Report Coordinator).

It is appropriate that some reports of wrongdoing are handled at the line-management level and no reporting or formal investigation action is undertaken. This can occur if

- the matter is minor and is normally dealt with at line-management level
- the matter has relevance only to the local work unit
- the number of parties involved is minimal
- no disciplinary or legal action is warranted
- the activity does not, on its face, indicate a wider pattern of behaviour in the organisation
- reprisal action is considered to be unlikely
- the reporter has been consulted and is satisfied that the matter does not proceed.

If line managers are in doubt about any of the above criteria, the matter should be recorded, notified and handled formally. Line managers who make the decision not to deal with the report formally should record the incident in accordance with the guidance above and retain the record.

Where the matter is covered specifically by another organisational policy—for example

- bullying and harassment
- personnel selection matters
- occupational health and safety
- breaches of professional practice

the report must be dealt with in accordance with those policies.

Investigation

All disclosures will be promptly and thoroughly assessed. Decisions as to the most appropriate action to be taken on the disclosure will also be made promptly.

The basis for these decisions will be fully documented.

Where a report warrants investigation, the Whistleblower Report Coordinator will arrange for that investigation to occur. The investigator will

- have appropriate skills and experience in investigation
- be independent of the reporter, other witnesses and any subject of the allegations

- as far as possible, protect the confidentiality of the reporter, any other witnesses and any person against whom allegations have been made
- conduct the investigation in accordance with procedures set down by the organisation.

If an internal investigation is to be conducted, terms of reference will be drawn up in order to clarify the key issues to be investigated. An investigation plan will be developed to ensure all relevant questions are addressed, the scale of the investigation is in proportion to the seriousness of the allegation(s) and sufficient resources are allocated.

Strict security will be maintained during the investigative process. All information obtained will be locked away to prevent unauthorised access.

All relevant witnesses will be interviewed and documents examined. Contemporaneous notes of all discussions, phone calls and interviews will be made. Where possible, interviews will be taped.

A report will be prepared when an investigation is complete. This report will include

- the allegations
- a statement of all relevant facts and the evidence relied upon in reaching any conclusions
- the conclusions reached and their basis
- recommendations to address any wrongdoing identified and any other matters arising during the investigation.

The principles of procedural fairness (natural justice) will be observed. In particular, where adverse comment about a person is to be included in a report, the person affected will be given an opportunity to comment beforehand and any comments will be considered before the report is finalised.

Risks of reprisal

The 'Sample policies and procedures' for Part D include detailed advice on the recommended risk-assessment process. This process needs to occur as soon as possible after the notification processes outlined above have occurred.

Confidentiality

Maintaining confidentiality is very important in the handling of a report of wrongdoing. Confidentiality not only protects the reporter against reprisals, it also protects any other people mentioned in or affected by the report.

Confidential information may include

- the fact a disclosure has been made
- any information that might identify the reporter or any person who might be the subject of a report of wrongdoing
- the actual information that has been disclosed in the report
- information relating to the disclosure that, if known, might cause detriment to any person.

When dealing with a report of wrongdoing, this organisation will fully comply with *(the relevant privacy legislation)*.

While every attempt to protect confidentiality should be made, there will be occasions when disclosure of the reporter's identity might become necessary.

These include

- providing natural justice to the person against whom the allegations have been made
- responding to a court order or legal directive (for example, subpoena, search warrant, notice to produce, direction by a parliamentary committee)
- court proceedings.

The reporter must be advised if their identity needs to be revealed for any reason listed above and the reporter's consent sought, where appropriate. The organisation will make all reasonable attempts to avoid a situation where identity will need to be revealed even though the reporter has not given consent. In protecting confidentiality, the organisation will ensure that the details of the report, the investigation and related decisions will be kept secure.

While the organisation should be prepared to take all steps necessary and appropriate to protect the confidentiality of the information that has been provided, the reporter also has some obligations. The reporter should not talk to colleagues or any other unauthorised person about the report and, in particular, disclose any information about the progress of the investigation.

Where confidentiality has been compromised, or is likely to be compromised, the organisation will, in consultation with the reporter, actively pursue strategies to limit any detrimental action and to support the reporter. This might include

- relocating the reporter to another work unit
- approving leave
- ensuring that other staff are aware of the consequences of initiating reprisal action
- openly acknowledging the organisation's commitment and support to the reporter.

Equity and natural justice

When the organisation receives a report of wrongdoing, it is often necessary to interview employees in the area where the suspected wrongdoing has occurred. An investigator appointed by the organisation will conduct these interviews. Persons who are the subject of a report of wrongdoing should be advised that

- they are encouraged and expected to assist the investigator
- if any allegations have been made against another officer, they will be notified formally about the nature of those allegations
- they may have a person of their choice present at the interview (for example, a colleague, peer support officer, confidant, union representative, legal representative or interpreter)
- they will be given an opportunity to make a statement, either orally or in writing
- if the allegations are referred to the police, they have a common-law duty not to obstruct them in their inquiries
- if in the course of the investigation evidence emerges that the subject of a whistleblowing report might be involved in the commission of a criminal offence, they will be informed of their legal rights
- where possible, their confidentiality and privacy will be respected.

Where it is determined that the whistleblowing report constitutes a false or misleading allegation, or that the report involves an unreasonable breach of confidentiality, sanctions will be applied against the reporter. These sanctions may be authorised by the relevant public interest disclosure legislation or some other authority.

D.

INTERNAL WITNESS SUPPORT

AND PROTECTION

I just think it's something we do so terribly bad at all levels. People are…more interested in covering their own tracks and keeping their own backsides clean, basically, than looking after the person who has reported the matter. The person who reported the matter is actually isolated into the 'baddie' situation. So they're not supported at all. All levels of organisation in the process tend to run away and make sure that they're not going to be getting into trouble for anything. That person that's reported it? Very isolated.
Manager

Support and protection of whistleblowers form the third—and arguably most important—objective of any whistleblowing program. The provision of organisational support to whistleblowers is, however, currently the single weakest area of most agencies' responses (Brown and Olsen 2008a). The bulk of agencies, in most jurisdictions, are urged to give active and urgent consideration to strategies for providing whistleblower support. In particular, agencies are encouraged to develop programs—commensurate with their own size and needs—for ensuring that support strategies are directed and, where necessary, delivered by persons with an institutional role that conflicts as little as possible with the challenges often implicit in providing that support.

Managers and case-handlers themselves were often unconvinced that their agencies had a very strong commitment to whistleblower support, and tended to have even less conviction that they were being effective in delivering that support. Table 4.1 indicates that both managers and case-handlers have quite an optimistic view about organisational commitment to protecting reporters. When it comes to effectiveness, while both are positive, case-handlers are a lot less positive than managers.

TABLE 4.1

The views of managers and case-handlers of the degree of organisational success

Issue	Case-handlers			Managers		
	Mean	SD	No.	**Mean**	SD	No.
Commitment of organisation to protecting reporters (1 = not at all strong, 5 = extremely strong)	**3.49**	0.99	340	**3.70**	0.90	535
Effectiveness of organisation in managing the welfare of reporters (1 = not at all effective, 5 = extremely effective)	**3.05**	0.91	338	**3.23**	0.83	532

Source: Question 59 of the Case-Handler and Manager Survey.

The interview data were more ambiguous on this issue. Managers and case-handlers (n = 34) were asked whether they thought their organisation was proactive or reactive in relationship to whistleblower protection. Thirteen indicated that they considered the organisation to be proactive, and 14 indicated that they considered the organisation to be reactive. The remainder did not offer an opinion.

Nevertheless, the results across the case-study agencies show that some organisations are considerably more successful than others in tackling this challenge. Figure 4.1 shows the varying proportions of all reporters (that is, of both public interest and personnel grievance matters) within each case-study agency who indicated whether, if they had their time over again, they would still report. While, overall, 82 per cent of reporters among the case-study agency respondents indicated that they were very or extremely likely to report again, this ranged from 64 per cent in Agency C to 90 per cent in Agency B (and 100 per cent in Agency P, noting the small number of respondents).

FIGURE 4.1

Likelihood of reporting again among all reporters by case-study agency (proportion)

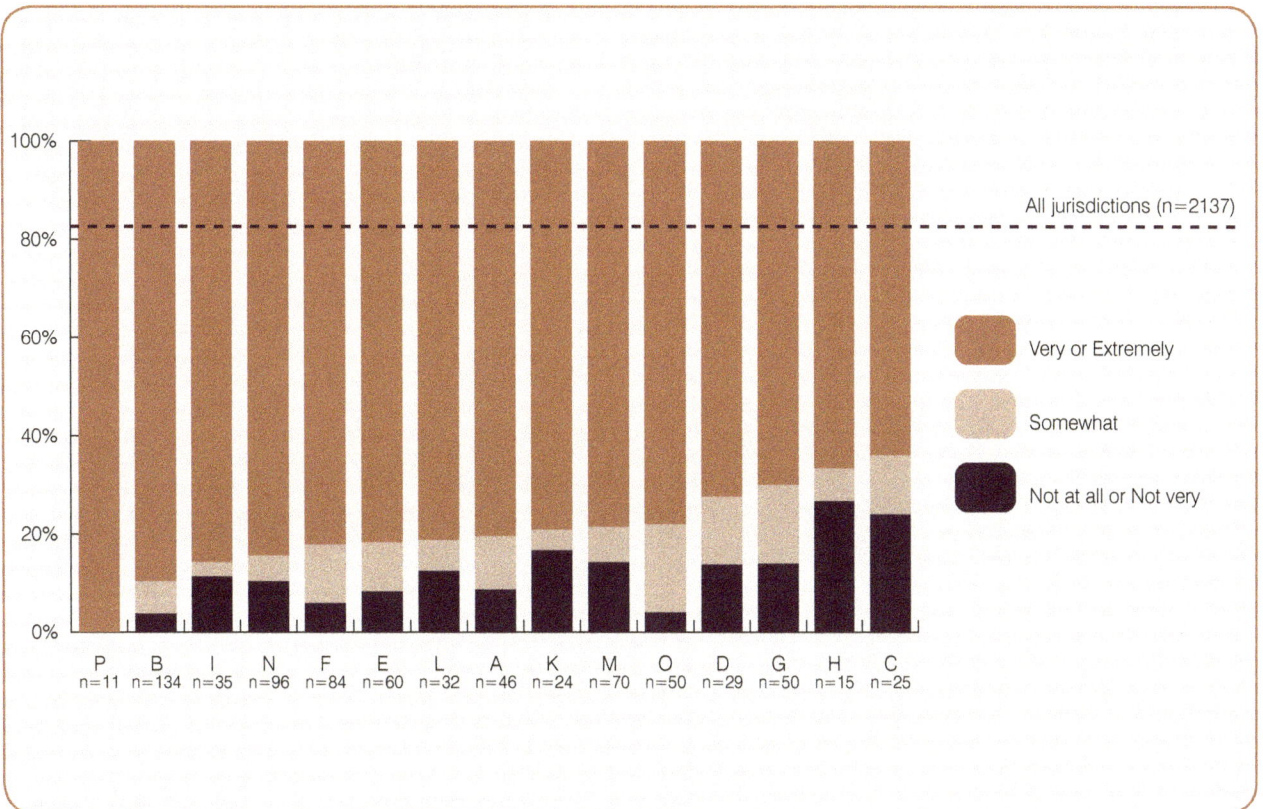

Source: Question 34 of the Employee Survey.

All agencies confront the dilemma of the appropriate scale, resourcing and organisational model of internal witness support. As pointed out in Section A3, commitment of resources is a key indicator of organisational commitment to the whistleblowing program as a whole. These practical issues of scale and model are addressed in Section E. Whichever options are chosen, evidence from across the case-study agencies points to common elements, all of which should be present in any organisation's approach in some form if the program is to have some prospect of success. This section outlines these elements.

The results from the research, interviews and case-study agency workshops confirm the direct and indirect benefits of more systematic approaches to the provision of support. Beyond simply the question of compliance with legislative mandate lies the reality that while positive or successful whistleblowing experiences often go unnoticed by the bulk of other employees in an organisation, negative outcomes can often become well known, costly and debilitating to organisational morale and performance.

There is a strong relationship between whistleblowers' perception about their treatment by the organisation and their stated willingness to report wrongdoing again (Smith and Brown 2008:127). While the factors influencing employees' stated willingness to report again are complex, the experience of the case-study organisations confirmed the importance of organisational support for preventing or minimising employee perceptions of mistreatment in many of the cases where support was provided.

An even more persuasive reason for providing support was confirmed to be the importance of disclosure experiences for defining whether the agency was able to deliver on commitments to provide its employees with a safe, healthy and productive workplace. A particular insight from the research was that internal support for whistleblowers is not necessarily a totally new or different strategy to other programs for maintaining or restoring healthy relationships within the workplace—even if it is often more complex than most other workplace health and safety issues.

The important relationship between organisational strategies for ensuring workplace health and safety and whistleblower support was recently confirmed in Victoria. There, Justice Judd of the Supreme Court confirmed that under that State's *Whistleblowers Protection Act 2001*:

> Detrimental action includes injury but importantly, extends to what may be described as collateral damage to a person's career, profession or trade, all of which may be apt to describe aspects of loss and damage suffered by employees...The breadth of the compensable loss and damage under the Act [means that], notwithstanding an overlap that might occur in the case of injury [under the *Accident Compensation Act*, the *Whistleblowers Protection Act*] creates a new, novel and additional class of rights and remedies to those which already existed...for work related injury.
>
> *Owens v University of Melbourne & Anor [2008] Supreme Court of Victoria No. 174 (27 May 2008) per Judd J*

No internal witness support strategy can hope to eliminate every case in which a whistleblower feels aggrieved—whether because employee expectations are simply unable to be met; because the degree of conflict between the employee and management becomes too great or insoluble; or because despite the best efforts, damage to a whistleblower's wellbeing or career is not able to be prevented. The experience in case-study agencies confirmed, however, that most agencies have both an opportunity and a responsibility to significantly reduce the number of employees falling into these categories. This would fulfil their obligations to their employees, lessen the costs of disclosure-related conflicts, and promote greater public confidence in their organisation's integrity.

D1. WHISTLEBLOWER/INTERNAL WITNESS SUPPORT

Checklist items

- A proactive support strategy for organisation members who report wrongdoing (that is, management initiated and not simply complaint/ concern driven), including

  - designation of one or more officers with responsibility for establishing and coordinating a support strategy appropriate to each whistleblowing case

  - support arrangements tailored to identified risks of reprisal, workplace conflict or other adverse outcomes.

- Risk assessment and support decision making that directly involves

  - the whistleblower(s) or other witnesses involved

- the identification and involvement of agreed support person(s) (for example, 'confidants', 'mentors', 'interview friends' or similar) with agreed roles.

DESIGNATED RESPONSIBILITIES FOR SUPPORT

The crucial lesson from the experience of case-study agencies was that decisions and responsibilities for the welfare of whistleblowers should not be left to chance. There was almost universal consensus that organised support for employees who report wrongdoing is vital to preventing or minimising the intra-organisational conflicts that can easily accompany reporting. The greatest difficulties were found among the many agencies where management responsibility for the provision of disclosure-related support was absent, confused and not backed up by the necessary resources.

> I just think it's something we do so terribly bad at all levels. People are...more interested in covering their own tracks and keeping their own backsides clean, basically, than looking after the person who has reported the matter. The person who reported the matter is actually isolated into the 'baddie' situation. So they're not supported at all. All levels of organisation in the process tend to run away and make sure that they're not going to be getting into trouble for anything. That person that's reported it? Very isolated.
> **Manager**

In making decisions about organisational obligations to provide support to whistleblowers, it is desirable to have a clear picture about where whistleblowers are likely to seek their support. The research project looked at this issue in some depth (Brown and Olsen 2008a:213–22). In summary, the project found that whistleblowers did not turn to the formal support structures in their organisation when they were experiencing a reporting incident. They sought their support from work colleagues (50 per cent) and family (44 per cent). Many sought support from the union or professional association (16 per cent). When making a report, the employee's supervisor was rated as the fifth most likely source of support (16 per cent) with formal internal support units rated twelfth. Where the reporting experience involved bad treatment, the pattern of support was broadly the same although formal internal support units were then used more frequently.

In brief, notwithstanding organisations' commitments to supporting whistleblowers, in practice, most whistleblowers leaned on family, friends and work colleagues.

As mentioned above, many reporters turned to their union or professional association for support. The issue was discussed frequently in the reporter interviews. Attitudes were evenly divided, with 14 reporters relating positive experience and 15 reporters relating negative experiences (n = 58). These organisations have the potential to provide significant support and benefit to reporters by advising on employment conditions and administrative review mechanisms, and providing personal support. Some reporters, however, expressed disappointment with the support they received from the union or professional association. These sources of support have resource limitations and, on occasion, are faced with the situation of one member reporting wrongdoing involving another member. That makes it very difficult for the union or professional association to meet the expectations of all parties.

Overall, managers and case-handlers were ambivalent about the effectiveness of their organisations in supporting reporters (Brown and Olsen 2008a:222, Table 9.1). While some were proud of their organisation's efforts, others were more critical. External agencies also have responsibility for the care and protection of those whistleblowers who choose to take their case to an external agency. Annakin (2011, p. 229) was critical of the preparedness and the capacity of those external agencies to fully protect and support those whistleblowers that came to them.

Further research into the adequacy of support mechanisms in organisations shows a similarly bleak picture.

- Support functions within organisations deal only with a small proportion of reporters. Crucial questions are posed by the research results about the size and reach of existing formal internal witness support programs. It is significant, however, that all 15 of the case-study agencies employing the respondents in Table 4.1 stated in their responses to Question 25 of the Agency Survey that they had systems and procedures for identifying internal witnesses in need of 'active management support', and nine of the 15 agencies indicated that they had a formal internal witness support program (Brown and Olsen 2008a:210).

- Most organisations rely upon employees needing support to actively self-identify (Brown and Olsen 2008a:211).

- Few agencies have even basic procedures for actively identifying internal witnesses who need support. When asked whether they had even basic procedures for identifying internal witnesses who might need active management support in Question 25 of the Agency Survey, 46 per cent of all agencies (n = 298) answered 'no'. Also, the analysis of procedures indicates that elements relating to support are weak (Roberts 2008:257).

- There is uncertainty in organisations about the best method of identifying employees who are in need of organisational support. When asked how internal witnesses accessed organisational support, no clear pattern emerged, with only 43 agencies or 23 per cent indicating that the agency took the initiative (n = 162, noting that 304 agencies responded to the Agency Survey) (Brown and Olsen 2008a:211, Table 9.5).

- Many agencies were reactive in the implementation of whistleblowing policies and procedures (including those dealing with support) rather than being proactive. In the interviews with managers and case-handlers (n = 34), participants were asked their opinion on whether the organisation was proactive when it came to handling reports of wrongdoing. Opinions were evenly divided: 12 described their organisation as being proactive, and 13 described their organisation as being reactive. Both managers and case-handlers were evenly divided on the issue.

A thread running through the analysis above is the reliance on employees to self-identify as needing support. This requires a high level of staff awareness of the availability of the support program, and for staff to self-identify not simply as a 'whistleblower', but as one unable to self-manage the situation. Many reporters deserving support might prefer not to access specialised support, at least initially, for fear of possible negative effects of being tagged as a whistleblower—a fear expressed by a number of the reporters interviewed. Staff who see whistleblowing processes as possible alternative means for pursuing a personnel or private grievance were more ready to try to enlist in such a program.

If agencies do not possess a sufficiently integrated system for tracking and notification of wrongdoing reports—discussed in Section C1—management runs the risk of being limited to a reactive approach, due to insufficient understanding of the level of whistleblowing within the organisation. This would mean reports being handled by supervisors and other managers in the first instance, with oversight or support occurring only after conflict arises.

> I think [the organisational culture] is fairly reactive. I think there's a lot of espousing of protection but the reality on the ground is that there is not a lot of protection that occurs.
> **Manager**

> And the next minute I'm sitting there and I'm home, and I didn't have a clue at that point. My marriage broke up, I lost my house. He even put in the affidavits for our separation that he was sick to death of me whingeing about [name of organisation]. There was a two-and-a-half-year property settlement because it was a very ugly bust-up. I lost my father, my job, my house, my partner. I thought, if I don't protect myself I'm going to crack. I don't believe that I did at any point. As far as Workcover were concerned, they thought I was suicidal. I'm sure they did.
> **Reporter**

SUPPORT ARRANGEMENTS TO ADDRESS IDENTIFIED RISKS

The adverse impact upon employees who come forward with reports of wrongdoing can be immense (Smith and Brown 2008:132, Table 5.16) and the likelihood of adverse effects is high (p. 123, Figure 5.1). This indicates the high risks of detrimental outcomes that surround public interest whistleblowing.

As with many other dimensions of the whistleblowing process, organisational performance varied significantly with respect to impacts upon reporters. Figure 4.2 shows the proportion of all reporters (that is, of both public interest and personnel grievance matters) from the case-study agencies who indicated adverse treatment, as well as those who indicated being treated the same or well.

FIGURE 4.2

Treatment by managers: all case-study agency reporters (proportion)

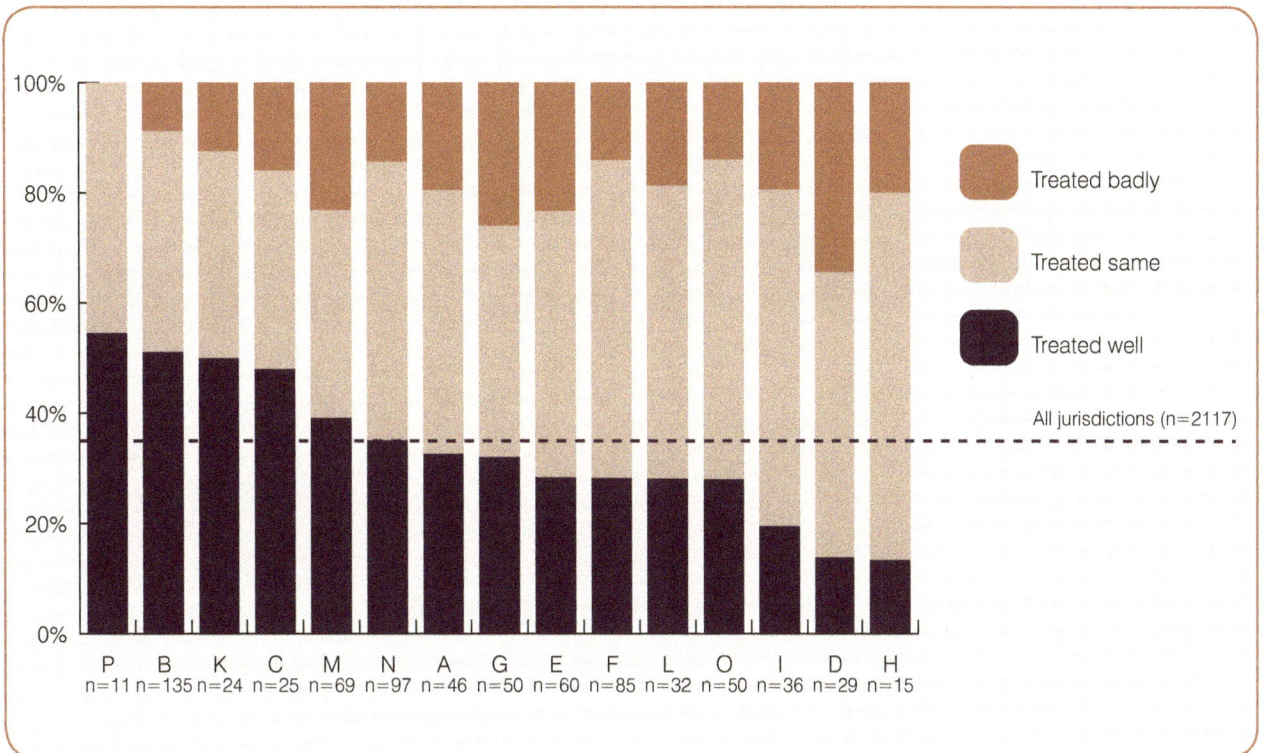

Source: Question 30 of the Employee Survey.

While the research project focused largely on the proportion of whistleblowers who reported being treated badly, the indicator presented here compares the case-study agencies on the positive measure of whether employees stated that they were treated well as a result of reporting. This was selected as providing a more objective indicator of good performance, since there is no guarantee that *any* employee will ever claim to have been treated well, but there might always be some employees who feel that they were treated badly even when objectively they were treated professionally.

For agencies to maximise the chance of performing well on such a measure, the research identified the importance of support strategies being designed to address the *actual* risks faced by most whistleblowers—as identified through the risk-assessment approach discussed earlier—rather than assumptions or stereotypes.

TABLE 4.2

Most common reported forms of adverse effect: whistleblowers, case-handlers and managers

Bad treatment or harm	Ranking by:		
	Whistleblowers	Case-handlers	Managers
Threats, intimidation, harassment or torment	1	1	1
Authority undermined	2	6	4
Illness	3	3	5
Motives for reporting questioned	3	4	3
Work heavily scrutinised	5	5	6
Ostracism	6	2	2
Forced to work with wrongdoers	7	9	7
Unsafe or humiliating work	8	14	20
Essential resources withdrawn	9	20	23
Missed promotion	10	10	10

Sources: Question 53 of the Internal Witness Survey; Question 48 of the Case-Handler and Manager Survey.

Table 4.2 ranks the top-10 adverse effects nominated by reporters, along with the rankings of managers and case-handlers who believed that the relevant type of harm had occurred at least once in the cases with which they had direct experience. A more complete list of adverse effects appears in Table 5.13 of the first report (Smith and Brown 2008:129).

These adverse effects could be interpreted to be low-level adverse outcomes, which many employees might normally be expected to endure and survive without difficulty. This would, however, be a superficial interpretation. The reality is that these outcomes are indicative of changes in the wellbeing and career of a whistleblower that might be extremely debilitating and destructive, and which every employer has a responsibility to prevent, minimise or address. This is especially the case because some outcomes might be inflicted passively or negligently by an organisation, simply through lack of organisational support or failure to assist managers to treat employees in a sympathetic way.

> I've gone through the phase where I've considered all the options and I had reached the conclusion that it was easier for me to kill myself and not put up with all this stress because by killing yourself you move what I call the 'stress conductor' into your family. The family suffers initially for a year or two, they're upset and stuff but generally they get over it and their lives continue, but as a whistleblower you just never get over it. It's always there.
> **Reporter**

TABLE 4.3

Feelings experienced by reporters (n = 220) as a result of whistleblowing (ranked in order)

Feelings	Scale	Mean	SD
Stress	1 = more stress to 5 = less stress	**1.73**	1.05
Trust	1 = decreased trust in organisation to 5 = increased trust	**1.77**	1.13
Frustration	1 = frustration to 5 = satisfaction	**1.78**	1.14
Betrayal	1 = betrayal to 5 = support	**1.89**	1.14
Anxiety	1 = anxiety to 5 = confidence	**1.91**	1.09
Power	1 = powerlessness to 5 = powerfulness	**2.03**	1.15
Persecution	1 = persecution to 5 = affirmation	**2.15**	1.15
Mood	1 = increased mood swings to 5 = decreased mood swings	**2.26**	1.03
Connection	1 = withdrawal from others to 5 = connection with others	**2.31**	1.13
Self-esteem	1 = decreased self-esteem to 5 = increased self-esteem	**2.54**	1.23
Self-worth	1 = decreased self-worth to 5 = increased self-worth	**2.65**	1.27

Source: Question 48 of the Internal Witness Survey.

It needs to be emphasised that, contrary to the views held by many, the most common source of adverse effects on reporters was mistreatment by management rather than by individuals or groups of co-workers (Smith and Brown 2008:121–7). When asked to rank what they considered to be the most likely adverse effect on reporters, managers overestimated the effect of ostracism by co-workers and underestimated the likelihood of poor treatment by management.

TABLE 4.4

Rating of treatment by managers and co-workers as perceived by whistleblowers, case-handlers and managers (mean)

	Treatment by managers (1 = extremely well to 5 = extremely badly)			Treatment by co-workers (1 = extremely well to 5 = extremely badly)		
	Mean	SD	No.	Mean	SD	No.
Non-role reporters responding to Employee Survey (all agencies)	**2.92**	1.04	1477	**2.67**	0.88	1457
Internal witnesses (case-study agencies)	**3.78**	1.14	222	**2.88**	1.08	218
Case-handlers (case-study agencies)	**3.11**	0.91	334	**3.38**	0.74	333
Managers (case-study agencies)	**2.72**	0.89	528	**3.23**	0.77	519

Sources: Questions 30 and 31 of the Employee Survey; and in the case-study agencies Questions 50 and 51 of the Internal Witness Survey, against estimates of treatment by case-handlers and managers; Questions 32 and 33 of the Case-Handler and Manager Survey.

Table 4.4 presents the mean rating of treatment by managers and co-workers as perceived by whistleblowers. Case-handlers appear to be fairly accurate in predicting the level of bad treatment by management, while managers underestimate the level of bad treatment by management. Both case-handlers and managers overestimated the degree of adverse effects caused by co-workers.

INVOLVEMENT OF IDENTIFIED SUPPORT PERSONS

The workshops of industry partners and representatives of the case-study agencies indicated that another key element in a successful support strategy is the availability of a wide range of potential support persons in the delivery of strategies to prevent and contain workplace problems associated with reporting.

A common primary objective of support strategies is, in effect, to create a network of persons around the whistleblower with the authority, skills and capacities needed to offset the risk of the individual suffering personal or professional harm. The anticipated harm can be both subjective (in terms of the stress of exposure to wrongdoing and/or the investigation process, and associated changes in self-image) and objective (in terms of actual likely conflict with colleagues, managers or the organisation as a whole).

By 'scaffolding' the whistleblower with additional psychological and professional infrastructure, support persons are expected to

- help identify and rationalise reprisal risks
- assist the whistleblower to cope
- help identify any actual emergent reprisals or problems, including early warning to management that confidentiality has ceased or been breached
- help identify when management intervention is needed in the workplace to address reprisal risks or other conflicts
- provide alternative, trusted avenues of communication between the whistleblower and investigators or managers (or both) at difficult times
- help provide workplace leadership among their peers, in response to conflicts
- provide ongoing support to help the whistleblower get back on an even keel
- provide independent verification of the decisions taken to manage the case, as well as the success or otherwise of the strategies adopted.

The responsibilities of support persons often complement the formal responsibilities of managers for the welfare of their employees (for example, supervisor, line manager, an internal witness support coordinator, case manager, human resource manager or CEO).

Organisations are urged to be creative in considering the potential sources of assistance that reporters use, noting the preferences of reporters as indicated in the table earlier in this section. One large case-study agency contracts former experienced managers of the agency (now retired) to provide mentoring-style support to whistleblowers on an as-needed basis. Some larger agencies also offer professional staff such as welfare officers, counselling staff or career development officers.

Within different agencies, two different types of non-specialist support person are sometimes acknowledged as having recognised roles in the process. Both are potentially relevant in any particular model of internal witness support, as discussed in Section E1.

- 'Confidants' or 'mentors' are experienced officers who volunteer and are vetted by management to be available to provide informal support to internal witnesses on an *ad-hoc* but formally recognised basis (especially from outside their normal workplace and line of management reporting).
- 'Peer support persons' are officers from within or close to the whistleblower's own workplace—for example, a trusted and capable friend—who are confirmed by internal investigators and the internal witness support coordinator as appropriate to be trusted with potentially confidential information in relation to the individual case.

The research suggests that only relatively few agencies are making use of practical, low-cost strategies such as this to deliver support in a formally recognised way. The case-study agencies that ranked best in the comparative analysis of outcomes were, however, conspicuous for having well-developed strategies of this kind.

PRACTICAL ACTION

It is recommended that organisations give priority to developing (or maintaining) effective systems for the receipt and notification of disclosures to ensure appropriate monitoring of and responses for internal witness support.

Ideally, at least one, and preferably more than one, manager within the agency should have a designated responsibility to provide—or coordinate the provision of—active management support to all whistleblowers in need or potential need. Those designated should have the appropriate capacity and expertise, and be appropriately positioned within the organisation to fulfil this role. In most circumstances, they will coordinate or share responsibilities for support with others, including line managers (see below). Further, it is suggested that they have formal responsibility for the provision of support, to deal with the complex and often high-conflict circumstances that might arise, and to ensure that management decisions in relation to the whistleblower are appropriately guided, monitored, adjusted and, where appropriate, initiated.

The workshops of industry partners and representatives of the case-study agencies indicated that it is important not only that support strategies are designed to address the actual risks faced by whistleblowers, but also that whistleblowers are actively involved in all key risk assessments and decisions regarding the support arrangements to be put in place around them. Effective communication, advice and feedback are vital ingredients in maintaining the wellbeing of whistleblowers. Of particular importance are ensuring that risk assessments are fully informed and accurate from the perspective of the whistleblower; that support strategies are well designed and operating with the whistleblower's consent; and that both the agency and the whistleblower have good records of the measures taken to prevent and contain workplace problems associated with their reporting.

Finally, it is recommended that whistleblowing support strategies draw on a network of potential support persons with the authority, skills and capacities needed to prevent and contain workplace problems associated with reporting. Two types of non-specialist support person roles—which complement the formal responsibilities of management—include confidants and mentors, or peer support officers.

D2. INFORMATION AND ADVICE

Checklist items

- Timely provision of information, advice and feedback to reporters and witnesses about

  • the actions being taken in response to disclosure

  • reasons for actions (including no action)

  • how to manage their role in the investigation process, including who to approach regarding issues or concerns regarding reprisals

  • ultimate outcomes, benefits to the organisation and remedial change.

- Provision of information, advice and access to

  • appropriate professional support services (for example, stress management, counselling, legal, independent career counselling)

  • external regulatory or integrity agencies that can be accessed for support.

INFORMATION, ADVICE AND FEEDBACK

Regular and accurate information, advice and feedback to internal witnesses on action being taken in response to their disclosure are crucial to the minimisation of real and apprehended risks of whistleblower mistreatment (Smith and Brown 2008:117–21). While noting that in many instances reports of wrongdoing are investigated and found to be lacking in substance, various organisations will meet the challenge to keep whistleblowers informed differently.

Figure 4.3 shows the variation between the case-study agencies as ranked by the proportion of all reporters (that is, of both public interest and personnel grievance matters) who knew whether their disclosure was investigated. The agencies are ranked according to the proportion who did not know one way or another, since while there might be a number of legitimate reasons why agencies might not investigate a report of wrongdoing (for example, lack of jurisdiction, or the matter does not warrant it), with the exception of anonymous reporting, there is little justification for agencies not informing whistleblowers of whether or not their report will be investigated. There was a strong correlation between agencies with a proportion at or below the national average and the agencies ranked as best performing against all whistleblowing outcomes.

> We weren't [informed], and I think that fed to our anxiety because, as I said, two or three weeks after we had reported it, we hadn't been told anything. We hadn't been told what was the next step; we hadn't been told where they were up [to] in the investigation—nothing like that. And as I said, that's why I went to see the [name of supervisory position], because I felt that I wasn't getting any input or any contact from the HR person. So I spoke to her about it, who then got him over and yeah, so no. Very poor—and that meant we felt that we would've perhaps managed it better if we had been better informed.
> **Reporter**

FIGURE 4.3

Knowledge of whether investigated: all reporters (proportion)

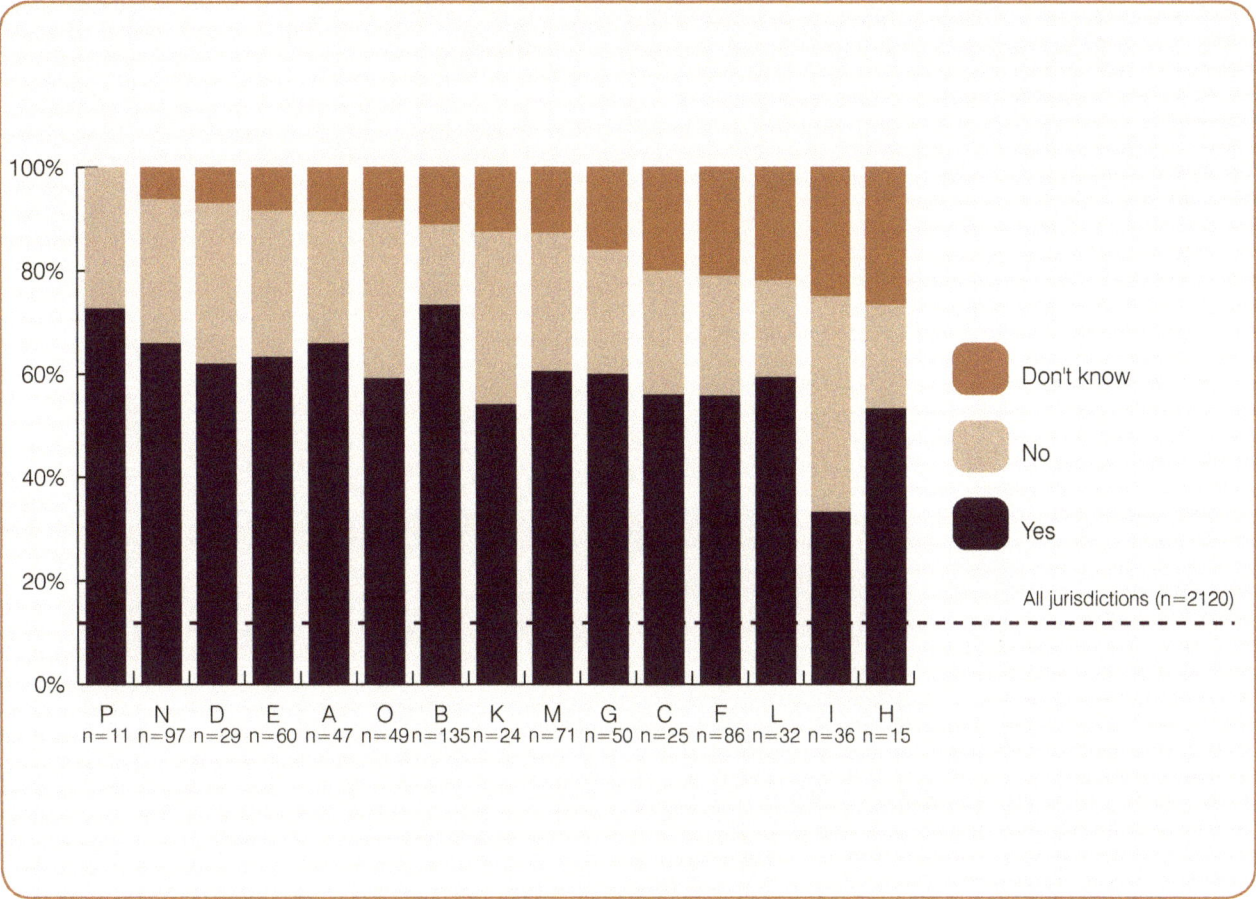

Source: Question 32 of the Employee Survey.

It is suggested that—whether or not the reporter accepts the validity of an unsubstantiated outcome—there is an obligation upon the organisation to report back to the whistleblower with the result and an explanation. While there might be a number of legitimate reasons why agencies might not investigate a report of wrongdoing (for example, lack of jurisdiction, or because the matter does not warrant it), with the exception of anonymous reporting, there is little justification for agencies not informing whistleblowers of whether or not their report will be investigated.

Notwithstanding that some organisations do better than others at informing reporters of outcomes, generally whistleblowers do not feel that they are being adequately informed of the outcome of their reports. Table 4.5 indicates the low levels of internal witness satisfaction with the amount of information that was provided to them about the investigation process.

TABLE 4.5

Internal witness perceptions of feedback

Issue (all scaled 1 = 'not at all' to 5 = 'extremely')	Mean	SD	No.
How well informed about progress of initial investigation	**2.05**	1.21	221
How well informed about outcome of initial investigation	**2.13**	1.25	220
How well informed about progress of further investigation	**2.15**	1.20	137
How well informed about outcome of further investigation	**2.11**	1.21	134

Sources: Questions 33, 35, 41 and 43 of the Internal Witness Survey.

For the internal witnesses who were interviewed, lack of feedback was a very common theme and was often associated—in the minds of the reporters—with the adverse effects caused by the whole reporting process.

MANAGING EXPECTATIONS ABOUT INVESTIGATIONS

The research confirmed the crucial importance of information being provided to reporters to help manage their role in the disclosure and investigation processes, including whom (and when) to approach regarding workplace issues or concerns. A central issue was that of managing whistleblowers' expectations regarding outcomes from an early stage.

As indicated in the reporter interviews, when an employee makes the decision to report wrongdoing, they usually have expectations of what is going to occur. Logically, those expectations are linked to the nature of the wrongdoing that has motivated the reporter. Expectations of reporters can be grouped into two broad categories

- that a particular employee in the organisation would be held accountable for their actions (these expectations can range from the target person having their employment terminated through to—a lot more benignly—training to do their job better)
- a change in policy, procedures or administrative practices.

Some reporters recognise, in hindsight, that their expectations were not realistic. The word 'naive' was used a number of times.

Managers of whistleblowing units highlighted the importance of sitting down with reporters early in the process (preferably while they are still at the stage of considering whether to report wrongdoing) to talk through their expectations, how realistic those expectations are, and the sorts of outcomes that they could expect. In particular, managers believed it was important to stress to potential reporters that, depending on the nature of the case, they should not share concerns with colleagues, and instead talk to investigators and support staff about with whom else they can and should discuss their concerns.

Such early intervention was particularly important where employees with a history of existing difficult relationships within the agency came forward indicating that they wished to make a disclosure. In those circumstances, it was important to identify early whether the reporters' expectations were unrealistic and manage the case accordingly.

> *I had no expectations. I didn't know what the heck I was doing.*
> **Reporter**

The workshops of industry partners and representatives of the case-study agencies indicated that line managers have a key responsibility in a successful program to manage these expectations. Of course, while the interviews indicated that there is always the potential for line managers to attempt to squash a report where the complaint relates to, or impacts upon, them, this highlights the importance of having multiple reporting pathways, as discussed in Section B.

ACCESS TO PROFESSIONAL SERVICES

Counselling is perceived as an almost universal solution for issues identified with whistleblowers. The interviews with managers and case-handlers contain frequent mentions of external counselling services being made available to whistleblowers to assist them with any problems that they might encounter. In Question 63 of the Case-Handler and Manager Survey, case-handlers (n = 253) and managers (n = 394) in the case-study agencies were asked to nominate improvements to handling of reports in their agencies. The availability of external counselling services was frequently mentioned as an improvement that could be made to organisational arrangements.

> *I would not trust the internal [name of organisation] system because my experience over recent years is just that it doesn't work. It doesn't support anybody and there's no outcome.*
> **Reporter**

While some reporters express appreciation for the effort of counselling staff, others are critical, and many are ambivalent. A common model for counselling services in the Australian public sector is to have outsourced qualified counsellors (that is, clinical psychologists), paid for by the organisation on a pay-by-use system. The capacity for these counsellors—being bound by confidentiality provisions—to involve themselves in the institutional resolution of issues is usually limited to providing the client with advice. It should be noted that, in the table earlier in this section indicating sources of support, counsellors were rated quite highly and their use increased markedly if the reporter experienced adverse treatment or harm.

While no case-handlers or managers opposed the use of trained counsellors and other additional support persons, many were critical of managerial colleagues who used such structures to avoid taking direct responsibility for the support or protection of reporters.

Agencies are also advised to consider extending arrangements for ensuring that whistleblowers can access other appropriate professional services, including legal support and independent career counselling support.

ACCESS TO EXTERNAL AGENCIES

The value of engaging relevant external regulatory or integrity agencies in the design and delivery of a whistleblowing program (Section A4) and the importance of advertising external reporting pathways to staff (Section B3) have already been discussed. It has also been suggested that agencies should ensure that their tracking and referral procedures for all significant reports of wrongdoing include routine notification to the lead integrity agency responsible for overseeing whistleblowing matters in their jurisdiction (Section C1).

These measures, along with others below, can help organisations share responsibility for the handling of whistleblowing matters in circumstances where there might be a high risk of conflict between the whistleblower and the organisation. This can occur even in agencies with elaborate support processes. If such circumstances arise, or fail to be successfully prevented, it is important that internal witnesses know that they may approach an independent oversight agency as a safety valve. Where possible, they should do so with the agency's support. It is recommended that governments ensure at least one coordinating integrity agency has the statutory authority and capacity to respond readily to such cases (Brown and Wheeler 2008:310).

A reporter can easily become concerned or dissatisfied if they feel they are being left in the dark or that nothing is happening. To ameliorate such concerns, managers, in consultation with specialist areas, could assure reporters

- that the organisation has assessed their information

- what the organisation has done or intends to do with the information

- the likely time frames involved

- their involvement in the process (for example, providing further information to investigators)

- the protections that will apply

- their responsibilities (for example, maintaining confidentiality)

- that their organisation will keep their identity confidential unless this is unreasonable or impractical

- how their organisation will update them on progress and outcomes

- who to contact if they want further information or are concerned about reprisals.

There is a reciprocal obligation upon the reporter to be prepared for what can be a difficult process. At the outset, it is suggested that the internal witness support area or a manager discuss with the reporter what outcome they want, and whether the organisation will be able to deliver.

Finally, organisations are urged to advise reporters of how to access any employee assistance or other counselling programs, as well as other relevant professional services.

D3. PREVENTING AND REMEDYING DETRIMENTAL ACTION

Checklist items

- Mechanisms for ensuring that
  - the welfare of organisation members who report wrongdoing is monitored from the point of first report
  - positive workplace decisions are taken for preventing, containing and addressing risks of conflict and reprisal
  - supervisors or alternative managers are directly engaged in risk assessment, support decision making and workplace decisions, to the maximum extent possible.
- Clear authority for support personnel to involve higher authorities (for example, CEO, audit committee and external agencies) in whistleblower management decisions.
- Specialist expertise for investigating alleged detrimental actions or failures in support, with automatic notification of such allegations to relevant external agencies.
- Flexible mechanisms for compensation or restitution in the event of any failure to provide adequate support, or prevent or contain adverse outcomes.

With few exceptions, public sector organisations are not good at recognising the potential for detrimental action arising from the reporting of wrongdoing (see Section D1). Therefore, there is a need for most agencies to strengthen their capacity to minimise risks of adverse treatment by management, including negligent adverse treatment, through a procedure for routine independent verification of the organisational position (for example, work performance) of employees who report wrongdoing, as close as possible to the time when they first report it.

The research confirms that in many whistleblowing cases, even when it is clear that adverse actions have been taken, agencies can have difficulty separating justified management actions from those that represent unjust or inappropriate action. It is clear that part of the difficulty in establishing whether the treatment of a whistleblower is or is not justified often lies in evidentiary difficulties as to whether particular problems associated with an employee's relationships with colleagues or supervisors commenced prior to, simultaneously with or subsequent to a disclosure issue arising.

POSITIVE WORKPLACE DECISIONS AND STRATEGIES

> *I use the word abrogation and I've used it in a couple of reports; I do think that [they] abrogate their managerial responsibilities to the EEO officer or to the probity and ethics officer or personnel or whoever else they can offload it [to].*
> **Manager**

A corollary of the risk-management and proactive-support strategy approaches discussed earlier (Sections C2 and D1) is that the support strategy will flow through to any necessary positive workplace decisions concerning the prevention or containment of risks of conflict or reprisal, before such problems arise.

Reprisals against persons who report wrongdoing are predictable in most organisational environments, as discussed in Section D1. The tendency in such circumstances can be for managers at all levels to 'back off and see what happens' before developing strategies to contain any likely detrimental outcomes. In many such cases, when conflict and stress eventuate, the fact that no strategy is in place to manage them (operationally, as against in theory) can contribute to an immediate sense of grievance on the part of whistleblowers, and a breakdown in trust with management, constituting real or perceived detrimental action.

In line with obligations to ensure a safe workplace, case-study agencies widely agreed that when confidentiality expired or was impossible, it was most desirable that agencies developed clear processes for when and how to intervene in workplaces to mitigate the risks of detrimental action (for example, by directly raising with supervisors or work units that reprisals would be frowned upon). This was seen as a different approach to many current arrangements whereby, even though everybody knows about the report, no-one says anything.

Equivalent active intervention might sometimes be needed to advise complainants or others about what action management is taking—notwithstanding fear of compromising the privacy and confidentiality of persons about whom allegations are made—and other actions to communicate what is happening in the organisation, to ensure that reporters do not wrongly interpret particular management actions as reprisals, and that others properly understand the pressures faced by participants in a whistleblowing process.

INVOLVEMENT OF LINE MANAGERS IN SUPPORT

A further corollary of the above approach is that arrangements need to be in place to ensure that supervisors or alternative managers are directly engaged in any support strategy and related workplace decisions, to the maximum extent possible in each case. This applies wherever confidentiality and investigation requirements permit, and where there is no conflict of interest in the provision of support (for example, where the employee's supervisor is implicated in wrongdoing or inaction). If there is, an alternative line of management supervision might need to be established.

A number of managers interviewed confirmed the view that having professional counsellors, particularly external counsellors, involved in support does not relieve line managers of their duty to support and protect their staff. Another dimension to this issue is that, unless positive arrangements are put in place to include line managers in the support strategy (where this is possible), some supervisors might willingly take the risk-averse course of assuming that their responsibility for the employee has ceased.

While it is logical to make a judgment that more resources need to be put into supporting whistleblowers, this is not the complete solution. One large public sector organisation with multiple physical locations adopted the practice of locating counselling services in regional hubs with a recommendation to its organisational units to refer personnel-type problems to those services. That policy was found not to be optimal and the organisation, while keeping the counselling services, eventually made its frontline managers in each organisational unit responsible for dealing with the issues. This highlights the inevitable conflict between having high-quality, consistent professional services remote from the workplace and the clear advantage of locally dealing with issues while accepting the problems of inconsistency that might accompany such an arrangement.

Another issue identified in the research was the need for organisations to provide training and support for managers themselves, to help them avoid risks of being seen to favour one or the other side (partisanship) in workplace conflicts. One manager pointed out that there was a fine line and that managers needed greater training and experience so as to be able to provide support without prejudging the case and treating the reporter either with such suspicion or with such approval that their direct involvement exacerbated the risks of conflict.

While no case-handlers or managers opposed the use of trained counsellors and other additional support persons, many were critical of managerial colleagues who used such structures to avoid taking direct responsibility for the support or protection of reporters.

EXPERTISE IN RESPONDING TO REPRISALS

As reported in the previous section, very few organisations have effective processes for identifying threats of reprisals through an effective risk-management process. Overall, agencies also do not deal well with reprisals or other detrimental action when it is alleged. (A major reason for this might be that detrimental action is often sourced to management itself, as noted in Section D1).

Those shortcomings are the following.

- Many organisations do not have specific policies for responding to reprisals against employees who report wrongdoing. (When asked whether they had formal procedures and policies for responding to reprisals against employees who had reported wrongdoing in Question 37 of the Agency Survey, 45.1 per cent of agencies said yes, 52 per cent of agencies said no, and 3 per cent did not respond; n = 304).

- Many organisations do not have staff with responsibility for ensuring that

> *I don't think we protect our employees particularly well at all and we don't really have line managers or HR managers that know how to do that protective function particularly well or inform employees of how that works. And so I think, often reprisals still occur because line managers, particularly, don't know how to protect staff.*
> **Manager**

> *I think the resources are there, I'm not sure we use them as effectively as we could. I think it's also beyond the formal resources. It's all very well to say 'well, we've got x number of bodies working in this area and we've got welfare and we've got this and we've got that'—they're not the issues. It's the general what happens on the floor in the workplace that really needs to be supported. So, all of those other things can happen, and they can happen really, really well because that's someone's job but unless they're supported back in the normal working environment and unless that happens well then the person's going to feel unsupported no matter what other resources were thrown at them.*
> **Manager**

employees who report wrongdoing are protected from reprisals. (In response to Question 38 of the Agency Survey about the staff responsible for ensuring that employees who report wrongdoing are protected from reprisals, 29.3 per cent of agencies indicated that no staff were identified, 30.6 per cent of agencies nominated investigations staff, 20.4 per cent nominated support staff, 32.6 per cent nominated the employee's supervisor or line manager, and 24 per cent nominated some other sort of support; n = 294. Note that agencies were able to nominate more than one source of support.)

- Those elements in whistleblowing procedures that deal with the support and protection of reporters are the least likely to be present (Roberts 2008:258).

- Where a whistleblower takes a matter involving reprisals to an external agency, it is not likely that they will experience effective action (Annakin, 2011, pp. 241-245).

- As indicated in Table 4.6, the views of managers and case-handlers indicated that they generally accepted that reporters were likely to experience problems but that their organisation was not particularly well equipped to deal with them.

TABLE 4.6

General views of managers and case-handlers on reprisals

Issue	Mean	SD	No.	Mean	SD	No.
Frequency of reporters experiencing problems from reporting (1 = never, 5 = always)	3.62	0.82	335	3.43	0.74	529
How well organisation deals with allegations of reprisals (1 = not at all well, 5 = extremely well)	2.89	0.99	331	3.03	0.90	510

Sources: Question 31 and Questions 34–36 of the Case-Handler and Manager Survey.

The workshops of industry partners and representatives of the case-study agencies identified the practical implications of the shortcomings discussed above as follows.

- Organisations often have difficulty distinguishing between what is reasonable management action and what the complainant considers to be some form of reprisal. In some circumstances, what are in fact reprisals are presented as reasonable action by management. In other circumstances, detrimental action might be taken in relation to an employee (for example, in a later workplace restructuring) without the full impacts of the decision upon the employee being understood by management.

- Organisations have difficulty distinguishing the linkage between performance issues and whistleblowing. Sometimes non-performing staff were left to continue on their course without any performance management action being taken. When there is a change in management, or some other trigger, action to increase performance can trigger a disclosure by the employee—which could be totally or partially designated as in the public interest. When an organisation finds itself in that situation, it has to rely upon prior documentation to verify the reporter's past poor performance and to demonstrate that the action management is taking is reasonable in the circumstances and would be taken against any employee whose work performance was the same. In other words, the management of reprisals is one aspect of the good management of staff.

- There can be an interaction between bullying and poor performance. The complainant might feel that bullying by management has caused their poor performance, while the management perspective is that their action was being taken to deal with poor performance. (An added complexity is that management action to deal with poor performance could be interpreted as bullying.)

- Current procedures in agencies tend to lead towards a lack of action for dealing with reprisals. Often the subject of an allegation is perceived as being dealt with by identifiable management action but any reprisals against the reporters are overlooked.

Where formal suspicions or allegations of detrimental action arise, many study participants confirmed that an adequate investigative approach is often not undertaken—because burdens of proof are too high, managerial actions are already too centrally implicated in what has occurred for an internal investigator to easily unpack the events, or because there is no-one sufficiently detached to fulfil the first criterion for an investigation of reprisal (complete independence from all action that has previously taken place).

Allegations of mistreatment are frequently associated with a lack of substantiation of the original disclosure (Smith and Brown 2008:115, Table 5.2). While in some cases this might be because an employee is dissatisfied with the outcome, in others it almost certainly indicates that, without vindication, an employee is or perceives themselves to be 'fair game' for detrimental action. In such circumstances, whistleblowers often also have a predictably reduced level of trust in internal investigators to resolve any reprisal allegations.

It is recommended that organisations make detailed and flexible agency procedures for reprisal investigations a clear priority (Brown and Wheeler 2008:302). It was also suggested to the research team that, where allegations of detrimental action arise involving senior managers, special arrangements are needed to engage independent investigators such as a senior retired officer familiar with the organisation and its processes. Independent integrity agencies also need to take a more prominent, early role in the investigation of detrimental action than currently occurs, or ensure close monitoring of matters flagged as high risk.

MAKING IT RIGHT: COMPENSATION AND RESTITUTION

The research established the need for flexible mechanisms for compensation or restitution where there is failure to provide reporters with adequate support, or to prevent or contain foreseeable adverse outcomes. Agencies need to develop new processes for recognising the detriment that reporters can suffer as a result of reporting wrongdoing. This issue is also a priority for legislative reform in all Australian jurisdictions. The first report made a number of recommendations for legislative reform (Brown et al. 2008a:271–7) and, as noted elsewhere in this guide, there have been legislative developments occurring within the context of these recommendations. The research team has urged legislatures in jurisdictions engaged in revising public disclosure legislation to recognise in future legislation the detriment that whistleblowers can suffer.

An issue that agencies are encouraged to explore is the usefulness of formal apologies to employees, or former employees, who reported wrongdoing and suffered adverse effects as a result of that reporting. In particular circumstances, a formal apology from the CEO can play an important part in putting the difficult situation faced by reporters behind them. This issue was discussed at length at the workshops of representatives from the case-study agencies and industry partners. One case-study agency has adopted the practice of giving formal awards to staff who come forward with reports of wrongdoing. These awards are presented at an annual ceremony where similar awards for exemplary performance are recognised.

In a hearing as part of the inquiry into the protection of whistleblowers by the House of Representatives Standing Committee on Legal and Constitutional Affairs, the National President of Whistleblowers Australia, Peter Bennett, noted:

> I would say that most people do not look for compensation. All they want to do is go back to the position they were in without a loss and accept a really nice, genuine apology. That is what most people would prefer.
>
> *(House of Representatives Standing Committee on Legal and Constitutional Affairs 2008:25)*

In addition to apologies, management failure to protect or support internal witnesses should be actioned through disciplinary measures, and in organisational assessments of the relevant manager's fitness to retain supervisory responsibilities.

A final issue concerns compensation by way of adjustments in career path, favourable transfers or access to allowances, or financial compensation for psychological damage and/or damage to career prospects. No jurisdictions have well-developed systems for awarding such forms of compensation to whistleblowers through existing grievance, workers' compensation or equality-of-opportunity processes. Until such systems are better developed, individual agencies are encouraged to consider their own options for bypassing or fast-tracking formal systems in order to facilitate compensation in deserving cases.

PRACTICAL ACTION

Procedures for the routine independent verification of the work performance of employees who report wrongdoing would ideally be complementary to those for the investigation of allegations about reprisals or failures. Such procedures are recommended as a proactive measure to help resolve later issues in cases when they arise, and as a preventive measure against unjustified actions being taken. Elements of such a procedure could include

- clear documentation as to when and how concerns about wrongdoing were first aired
- collection by a relevant investigator of the evidence existing at the time of the report regarding the reporter's work performance and relationships, undertaken with the knowledge and participation of the reporter
- where a report is still confidential, alternative strategies such as a general audit of the work histories of all employees in the relevant section to establish the relative position of the employee, in parallel with the primary investigation.

Organisations are encouraged to ensure that their support systems are triggered automatically and operate proactively to prevent or mitigate risks of reprisal or other workplace conflict. For example, organisational policies and procedures could clearly state

- that managers and supervisors are responsible for dealing with issues that arise in their workplace and for providing support to staff who report wrongdoing, regardless of any authority that rests with specialist areas such as a formal internal witness support unit
- when and how to intervene in workplaces to prevent detrimental action
- how reprisals against employees who reported wrongdoing will be investigated or otherwise dealt with
- when to communicate with reporters about what action the organisation is taking
- when formal apologies or compensation should be given to employees or former employees who report wrongdoing and suffer adverse effects as a result.

Logically, investigators of detrimental action will also require the skills, and authority, to determine the essential facts of inherently complex allegations and counter-allegations, to have a sophisticated understanding of how organisations operate at a senior level, and to be able to make reasoned assessments of when an organisation might have fallen down in its responsibilities to prevent or contain workplace problems, even if specific, deliberate reprisal action cannot be proved or is not an issue.

The issues described above are further clarified in the 'Sample policies and procedures' at the end of this section.

D4. EXIT AND FOLLOW-UP STRATEGY

Checklist items

- Exit strategies for concluding organised support to whistleblowers.
- Follow-up monitoring of whistleblower welfare, as part of regular evaluation of programs and to identify ongoing, unreported support needs.

EXIT STRATEGIES FOR FINALISING WHISTLEBLOWING CASES

During the surveys and interviews, both managers and case-handlers recognised the importance of exit procedures for signalling the end of the reporting process, and marking the point at which support moves from an active to a monitoring phase.

TABLE 4.7

Value of exit and closure procedures

Issue	Case-handlers			Managers		
	Mean	SD	No.	Mean	SD	No.
Value of exit or closure procedures to reporter (1 = not at all valuable, 5 = extremely valuable)	**3.71**	0.97	98	**3.68**	0.83	145
Value of exit or closure procedures to organisation (1 = not at all valuable, 5 = extremely valuable)	**3.69**	0.96	98	**3.60**	0.85	145
Proportion of reporters able to put the matter behind them (1 = none or almost none, 5 = all or almost all)	**3.15**	1.30	319	**3.07**	1.33	487

Note: Respondents were only asked to rate the first two statements if they indicated in a previous question (Question 51) that their organisation used exit or closure procedures after investigation and management action ceased.

Sources: Questions 53–55 of the Case-Handler and Manager Survey.

Table 4.7 indicates case-handlers and managers are generally positive about the value of exit and closure procedures. Information from the agencies presented a much bleaker picture. Question 33 of the Agency Survey asked whether agencies had a formal exit or closure procedure for internal witnesses when they ceased to receive active management support. Of those agencies with some form of procedures for identifying internal witnesses who might need active management support (n = 160), 65.6 per cent indicated that they did not have exit procedures, 12.5 per cent indicated that they conducted formal exit interviews, 19.4 per cent indicated that they sent a formal letter to internal witnesses and another 14.4 per cent indicated that they had some other sort of procedure. When asked to describe these other procedures, agencies most commonly responded that they had informal processes that were undertaken on an ad-hoc basis. (Note that agencies were able to nominate more than one procedure.)

> *I feel like there's still no closure with the whole thing. But it's a huge toll to myself. My health has never been more—I've had to take time off. My wife had to take time off. We've been sick and if you look at our records we've never been sick up until four or five years ago when all of this happened. It's obviously affected my work as well but we're still trying to work as hard as we can at that school.*
> **Reporter**

In keeping with other findings in this area, however, the research identified shortcomings in the way in which organisations dealt with exit strategies. Only a minority of organisations demonstrated that formal exit procedures were regularly used. Question 58 of the Internal Witness Survey asked internal witnesses (n = 253) about the procedures that were used to mark the end of their involvement in the whistleblowing processes: 35.2 per cent of reporters said that no procedure was utilised; 4.7 per cent met with a manager; 7.9 per cent received a formal letter or communication; and 13.8 per cent nominated some other procedure. Regardless of whether or not organisational exit procedures are in place, such a response from internal witnesses indicates that they are not being fully utilised.

While one purpose of exit procedures is to facilitate closure for reporters and to enable them to get back to being fully productive members of the organisation, whistleblowers can also experience a great deal of difficulty moving on from the adverse effects of the reporting process.

> **Interviewer:** *Has there been any closure?*
>
> **Reporter:** *Oh absolutely not... There is no closure ever when dishonest people get away with their corrupt conduct and the very bodies which are there to protect our society and keep us going... are incredibly corrupt. When those bodies don't do their job there is never any closure.*

- Question 59 of the Internal Witness Survey asked internal witnesses (n = 253) about whether the whistleblowing experience was behind them: 37.5 per cent indicated that the matter was still very much with them; 11.6 per cent said that the matter was partly behind them, but they still had issues to deal with; 24.6 per cent said the matter was almost completely behind them, but they still had issues to deal with; and 26.3 per cent said the matter was completely behind them.

- In the interviews with reporters (n = 58), participants were asked whether or not they had moved on from the whistleblowing event. Of those who responded to the question, 43.1 per cent said that they had not moved on; 17.2 per cent indicated that they had moved on; and 10.3 per cent were undecided. Of those who said that they had put the events behind them (n = 10), four had left the work area, another four indicated that their report had been vindicated and two noted that the person about whom they had complained had left the work area.

Those interviews with internal witnesses indicated that, while some had moved on with their lives, many were struggling to put the whistleblowing experience behind them. Asking internal witnesses about closure often brought out the bitterness, helplessness and frustration they felt. Many managers and case-handlers indicated empathy for those reporters who could not put the matter behind them.

ONGOING MONITORING OF THE WELFARE OF INTERNAL WITNESSES

Few agencies undertake follow-up or monitoring of the welfare of internal witnesses after they have ceased to receive active management support. Question 34 of the Agency Survey asked whether agencies undertake follow-up or monitoring of the welfare of internal witnesses after they have ceased to receive active management support: 18 per cent of all agencies (n = 304), and 35 per cent of agencies with internal witness support procedures (n = 156), indicated that they did so. Those agencies were asked to briefly describe the follow-up or monitoring that they undertook. The most commonly mentioned responses were external watchdog agencies, unions and external counselling services. Very few organisations indicated that they used internal resources to monitor the wellbeing of internal witnesses.

Problems can occur for internal witnesses long after the report is made. This might be either direct (for example, where a report of wrongdoing results in a person involved in the wrongdoing returning to the workplace after a period of absence) or indirect (for example, long-term decline in a whistleblower's career prospects due to the desire to avoid stress and conflict).

Organisations should not automatically assume that all internal witnesses should be followed up indefinitely, even after the situation has been resolved. Some internal witnesses might not wish to be continually reminded of a difficult and unpleasant episode in their careers and would prefer to get on with their everyday work. Based on discussions from the workshops of representatives from the case-study agencies and industry partners, a preferable approach from the perspective of internal witnesses is for the organisation to provide them with an open-ended assurance of assistance and then for the internal witness to raise it with the organisation (usually a central whistleblowing support unit) if any further assistance is required.

> *I don't know that anybody actually does get closure from it. I think they're pretty much scarred and it does scar. It absolutely does scar and I think that in all future dealings there'd be that experience in mind in the way they tackle problems, or if they had to do the whole thing all over again they'll say, you know what, I won't. So yes, I think that will be their ongoing [issue] and I don't know that the mechanisms in place deal with no closure at all.*
> **Manager**

PRACTICAL ACTION

Ongoing monitoring, rather than interventionist follow-up, appears to be a preferable option. Given the proportion of reporters who suffer adverse consequences, and the subtlety of those consequences, organisations do have an active responsibility to monitor the medium to long-term outcomes for whistleblowers. Organisations are encouraged to regularly engage in the follow-up monitoring of whistleblower welfare, as part of the regular evaluation of their program, and identify any ongoing needs.

SAMPLE POLICIES AND PROCEDURES

Whistleblower/internal support and protection

All persons who manage staff in the organisation have the primary responsibility for dealing with whistleblowing issues that arise in their work unit, including the support of those who report wrongdoing and protection for those persons from reprisal action. Those responsibilities exist regardless of any authority that rests with specialist areas, such as (name of organisational support unit).

Support strategy

The organisation should formally designate a senior officer as Whistleblower Support Officer (or some other designation in accordance with organisational nomenclature) who is responsible for initiating and coordinating action to support persons who have disclosed wrongdoing, particularly those who are suffering any form of detriment as a result. The name, position title, location and contact details should be included in references to that position in the procedures.

The function of the Whistleblower Support Officer should be separate from the investigation function. The role of the Whistleblower Support Officer is to

- provide moral and emotional support
- provide career advice to the whistleblower
- advise the whistleblower about any resources available in the organisation to handle any concerns that they might have as a result of reporting
- appoint a mentor, confidant or other peer support officer to assist the whistleblower

throughout the process

- refer the whistleblower to the organisation's employee assistance program or arrange for other professional counselling
- generate support for the whistleblower in their work unit (if appropriate)
- be alert to possible victimisation or harassment of whistleblowers and report any suspicions to the Whistleblower Report Coordinator
- maintain contact with all identified whistleblowers in the organisation and monitor their progress
- negotiate with the whistleblowers and their relevant supervisor a formal end to their involvement in the support and protection program, when it is agreed that they no longer need assistance.

Persons who have disclosed wrongdoing or are contemplating such disclosure should be formally advised that they will be provided with access to any necessary professional support, such as stress management or counselling services, or legal or career advice, which might become necessary as a result of the reporting process. The access point for this assistance should be the nominated Whistleblower Support Officer.

All managers in the organisation should be under an active obligation to notify the Whistleblower Support Officer if they believe any staff member is suffering any detriment as a result of disclosing wrongdoing.

Risk assessment

Whenever any manager in this organisation receives a report of wrongdoing, that person is under an obligation to consider the likelihood of the person making the report suffering some form of reprisal as a result. If relevant, that assessment should be extended to any other witnesses who are likely to be involved in the investigative process.

It is the responsibility of that manager to assess the actual and reasonably perceived risk of victimisation or unlawful discrimination. If that risk is significant, a risk assessment must be undertaken.

The process of risk assessment must include input from the person making the report. Having assessed the risk, that manager is responsible for notifying the Whistleblower Report Coordinator. Consistent with the level of assessed risk, the organisation will implement arrangements to protect the staff member who made the report and, where practicable, their anonymity.

Where necessary, the risk-assessment process might need to be repeated.

At all stages in this process, the organisation will keep the staff member informed. Also, all managers in this organisation have an active obligation to report to the Whistleblower Report Coordinator any reports they receive that indicate that action against a staff member in reprisal to a report is occurring. They also have an active obligation to report any suspicions they might have themselves that action against a staff member in reprisal to a report is occurring.

Information and advice

Any member of staff who makes a bona fide disclosure of wrongdoing is entitled to feedback. This feedback will include the following.

At the outset

- acknowledgment of receipt of the disclosure, as soon as possible but, in any event, within two weeks
- the time frame within which they will be advised of action to be taken
- the name and contact details of a person who will be able to advise them on what is happening—most appropriately the Whistleblower Support Officer.

After a decision is made as to how their disclosure will be dealt with

- the action that will be taken on their disclosure
- likely time frames for any investigation
- protections that will apply
- procedures in place to manage confidentiality; if confidentiality is unlikely to be maintained, the reporter should be advised and asked whether the reporter wishes to proceed with the report
- the resources available within the organisation to handle any concerns that they might have arising from the process of reporting wrongdoing, including the contact details of the Whistleblower Support Officer
- external regulatory or integrity agencies that they may access for support if they consider that they need support outside the organisation.

During the course of any investigation

- the ongoing nature of the investigation
- progress and reasons for any delay
- advance warning if their identity is to be disclosed.

At the completion of any investigation

- sufficient information (preferably in writing) to demonstrate that adequate and appropriate action was taken and/or is proposed in respect of their disclosure and any systemic issue brought to light
- advice as to whether s/he will be involved in any further matters—for example, disciplinary or criminal proceedings.

Within 90 days of any disclosure, the discloser will be informed of the action taken, or proposed, as a result of the disclosure, and the reasons for this decision. If the action has not been finalised within 90 days, the discloser will be informed when the proposed action is completed.

Preventing and remedying detrimental action

Commitment to protect

Persons who make disclosures have the right to request that the organisation take positive action to protect those persons against reprisals.

Protection mechanisms

The formal procedures for assisting persons making a report should include

- notifying whistleblowers that they should inform the Whistleblower Report Coordinator or the CEO immediately of any reprisal action
- reminding all managers in the organisation that they have an active obligation to notify the Whistleblower Report Coordinator or the CEO of any allegations they receive that indicate action against a staff member in reprisal to a report is occurring
- all managers in the organisation have an active obligation to report any suspicions

they might hold themselves that reprisal action against a staff member is occurring.

Where the Whistleblower Report Coordinator becomes aware of reprisal action against a whistleblower, the Whistleblower Report Coordinator will

- take immediate steps to ensure a senior and experienced officer who has not been involved in dealing with the initial report will investigate the suspected reprisal

- transmit the results of that investigation to the CEO for a decision

- take all possible steps to protect the reporter or internal witness

- where it has been established that reprisal action is occurring against a whistleblower, all steps possible must be taken to stop that activity and protect those parties

- appropriate disciplinary or criminal action will be taken against anyone proven to have taken any action in reprisal for the making of a report.

The reporter should be kept informed of the progress of the investigation and the outcome.

The CEO may issue specific directions to assist in the whistleblower's protection from any of the actions mentioned above. The nature of the action is dependent upon the circumstances and seriousness of the reprisals that the whistleblower is likely to suffer. The possible action that could be taken includes

- issuing warnings to those alleged to have taken detrimental action against the whistleblower

- relocating the whistleblower or the subject officer within the current workplace

- transferring the whistleblower or the subject officer to another position to which the whistleblower or they are qualified

- granting the whistleblower or the subject officer a leave of absence during the investigation of the disclosure.

The actions listed above will be done only with the agreement of the whistleblower, the Whistleblower Report Coordinator and the Whistleblower Support Coordinator. The Whistleblower Report Coordinator will make it clear to other staff that this action was taken at the whistleblower's request, with management support and that it is not a punishment.

Where another staff member comes forward as an internal witness to assist in the handling of a whistleblower report, and that person is threatened with or suffers some form of retaliation, that person is entitled to the same protection as outlined above.

Compensation or restitution

Where retaliation against a whistleblower or internal witness has been proven, the organisation will consider the payment of compensation, restitution or the making of a formal apology.

Exit and follow-up strategy

Where a report of wrongdoing has been actioned, the Whistleblower Support Officer, in consultation with the Whistleblower Report Officer, will develop and implement a plan for the monitoring of the wellbeing of the reporter (or internal witness, if appropriate) including a clearly defined exit strategy. The reporter (or internal witness) will be consulted as to the level and the nature of ongoing support.

E.

AN INTEGRATED

ORGANISATIONAL APPROACH

It's not about what they're doing right and wrong. It's a whole-department approach, and it is about having the money and strategies in place to be able to provide that support.

Investigator

Roberts | Brown | Olsen

As outlined throughout this guide, the three major objectives of a whistleblowing program are to encourage employee reporting of wrongdoing; ensure effective assessment, investigation and action of reports; and support and protect whistleblowers. While these aims must be underpinned by organisational commitment to the program, as described in Section A, our research has also confirmed the lessons from the previous sections that the effective operation of a whistleblowing program relies on a positive workplace culture and shared responsibilities, supported by dedicated resources.

Organisational commitment to the program must move beyond procedures setting out the responsibilities and obligations that must be fulfilled by staff to an approach that also emphasises the responsibilities of the organisation as a whole, including the most senior management. Examples of an integrated approach to embedding the whistleblowing program in everyday actions include

- explicit observations by management that reporting wrongdoing is in line with the organisation's ethical culture (as expressed in the code of conduct or equivalent mechanism), as well as being in accordance with the expectations of government and the public interest

- all levels of management setting a personal example by supporting staff who come forward with reports of wrongdoing and 'owning' the report

- with their consent, publicly acknowledging particular staff who have come forward with reports of wrongdoing

- building an understanding of whistleblowing processes through formal training mechanisms

- linking the treatment of staff who come forward with reports of wrongdoings to the assessment of the competence of managers.

Our research into the case-study agencies confirmed the value, on the whole, of more organised and proactive whistleblowing programs. The following elements are intended to ensure that the many complex issues involved in embedding a whistleblowing program in the organisation are addressed in a holistic fashion.

E1. CLEAR ORGANISATIONAL MODEL FOR SUPPORT

Checklist items

- Clear information about the support strategies employed by the organisation (that is, 'standing', 'devolved', 'case-by-case').
- Clear understanding of whistleblowing-related roles and the responsibilities of key players, internal and external to the organisation.
- Operational separation of investigation and support functions.
- Clear authority for support personnel to involve higher authorities (CEO, audit committee and external agencies) in whistleblower management decisions.

'Standing program'

This model includes a permanently staffed internal witness support unit to coordinate protection and support. This model is typical of some larger agencies. The shaded boxes indicate the primary network of responsibility for support.

As discussed in Section A3, resources are a key indicator of organisational commitment to any program. All agencies face the challenge of identifying what level of resources is commensurate with need, depending on the type of program chosen. Our research identified three broad choices of organisational model for the development of the internal witness support strategies that form the missing heart of most current programs. Figures 5.1 and 5.2 summarise the first two choices.

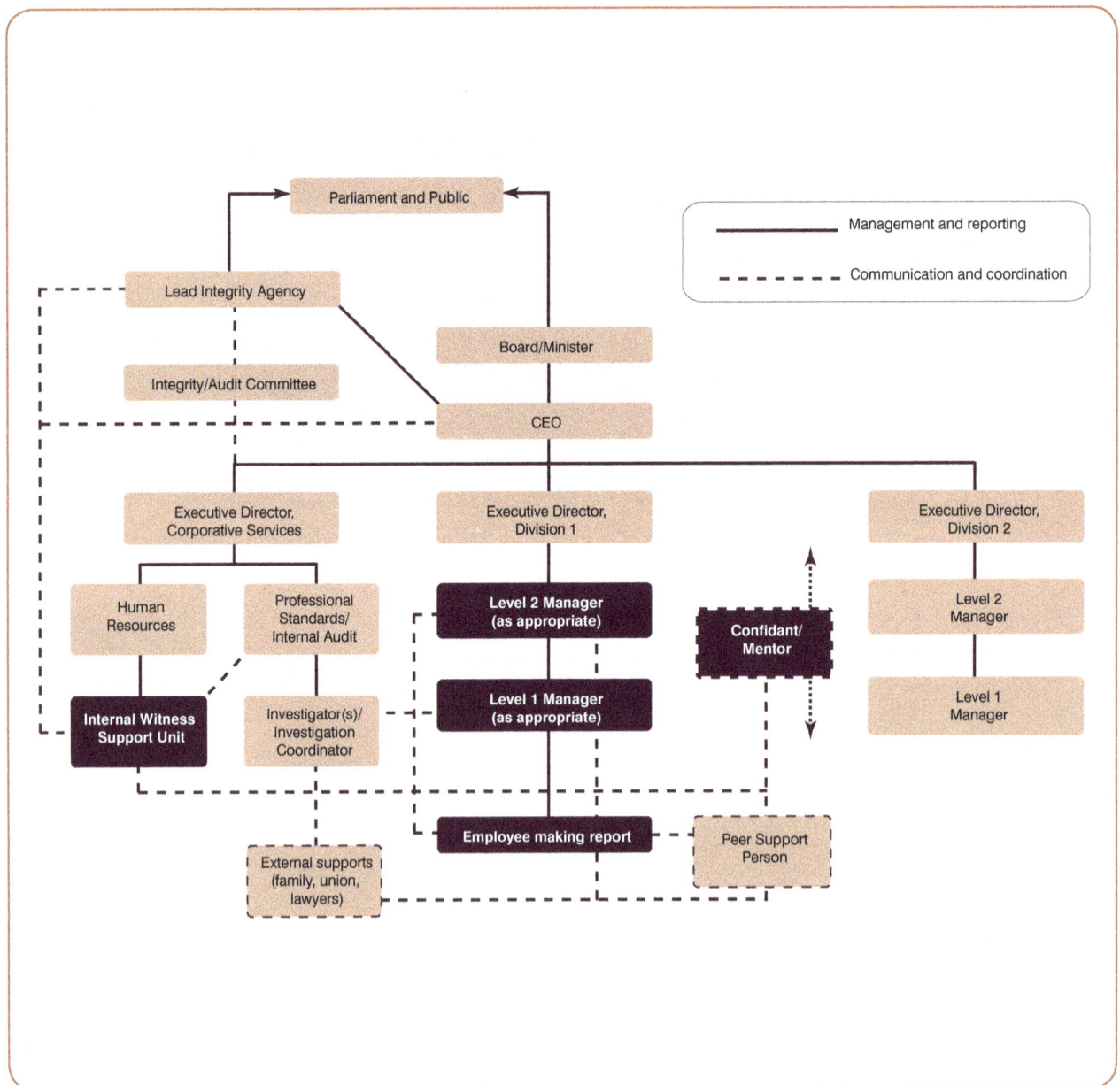

FIGURE 5.2

'Devolved program'

This model does not include a permanently staffed internal witness support unit, but assumes that the professional standards area of the organisation will provide coordination. This model is similar to those found in mid-sized agencies. The solid box around the 'confidant' indicates a more intensive and structured role than in the standing program.

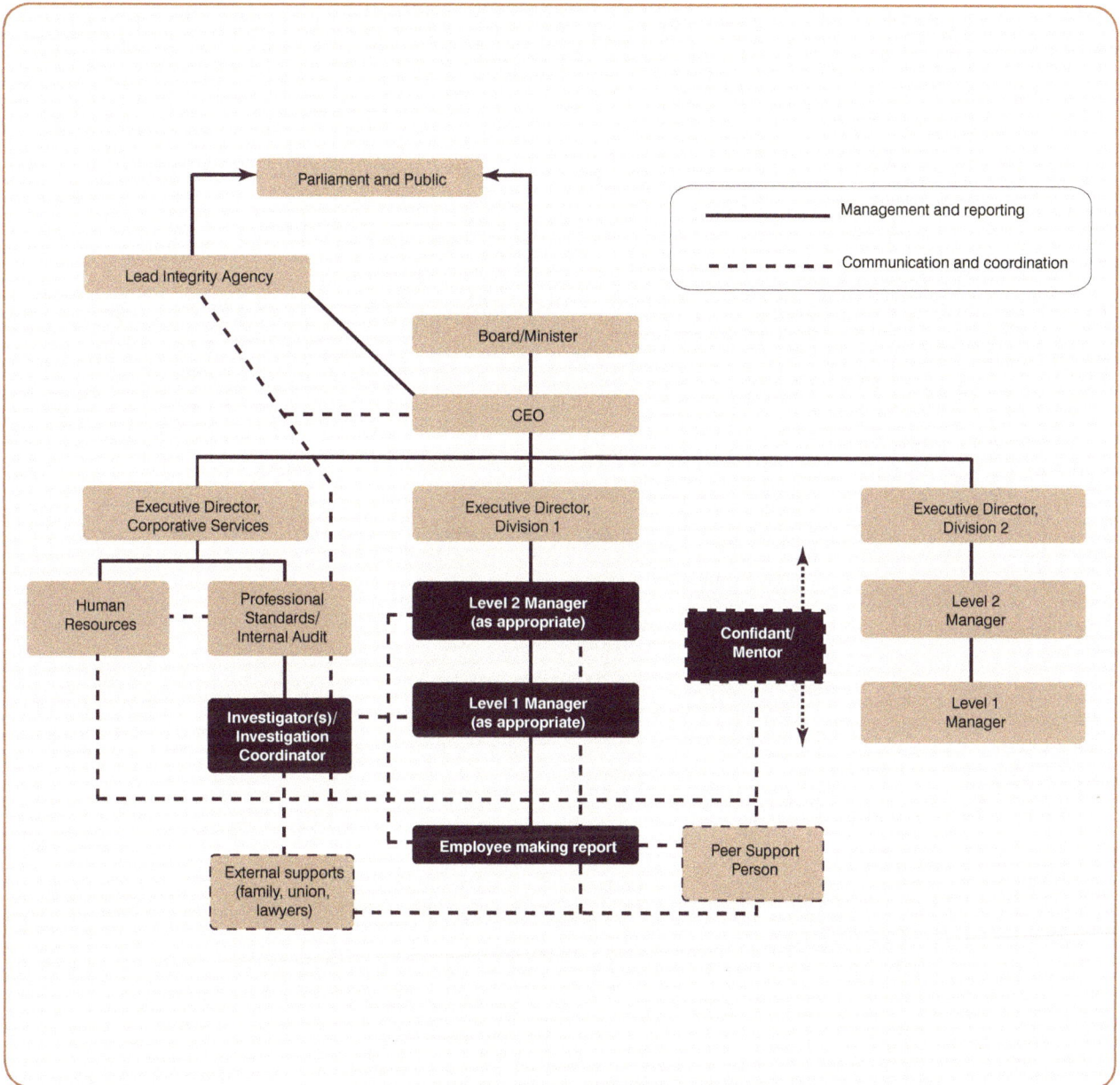

A **'case-by-case program'** involves similar actors but presumes that all involved, including a confidant, will be appointed on an as-needed basis rather than being part of an existing program. It is often the default choice for small agencies.

Other features of communication and reporting implicit in any of the programs are mentioned below. All three models presume a sharing of support responsibilities across various parts of the organisation, as well as external lines of communication (which are likely to become more significant and direct the less formal is the program). The typical roles of a 'confidant' and a 'peer support' person were described in Section D1.

Each model requires resource commitments, including for additional costs such as external counselling support on an 'as needed' basis, although the case-by-case model presumes that the appropriate skills and responsibilities are held by generic staff (such as human resource managers, or internal investigation unit employees) rather than dedicated staff.

Agencies need to determine a target case load for anticipated delivery of support, based on reliable evidence of reporting patterns within their organisation. (An associated issue is the need to anticipate the impact of changes in government policies on whistleblowing, particularly changes in legislation.) As previously reported, in the case-study agencies, perhaps only 1.3 per cent of all public interest whistleblowers were receiving organised support at the time of being surveyed (Brown and Olsen 2008a:208–12). This is despite the fact that, across the case-study agencies, on average, 20 per cent of whistleblowers went on to report having been treated badly by management or colleagues (giving an estimate in the order of 7700 individuals across the whole Australian public sector). While the estimated size of the 'at risk' population can be further refined in various ways, on any analysis the gap between the number of employees provided with organised support and the likely number of whistleblowers in need was very large.

For the purposes of estimating target need, agencies can use empirical research such as that presented in this report to identify the number of employees believed to be reporting wrongdoing, as well as the proportion currently experiencing negative outcomes. As a rough estimate, for example, our research shows that 12 per cent of all employees in an average agency reported public interest wrongdoing over a two-year period (Brown et al. 2008b:38, Figure 2.2), and on average 22–25 per cent of those perceived themselves as having been mistreated (Smith and Brown 2008:123, Figure 5.1).

If current levels of organised support were increased from less than 2 per cent of reporters to 10 per cent, and targeted to the highest-risk cases as identified through a risk-management approach, the prospects of significantly reducing the proportion of aggrieved whistleblowers should be high. For an agency of 10 000 employees, this estimate would amount to 120 employees over a two-year period.

CLEAR UNDERSTANDING OF ROLES AND RESPONSIBILITIES

Many of the elements of a whistleblowing program discussed in the previous sections involve relationships that cut across normal organisational lines and involve a wide range of individuals. It is important that these roles and responsibilities are clearly articulated in written procedures and explanatory materials, and reflected in formal position statements.

Figure 5.3 sets out one overview of how key responsibilities might by distributed across the organisation and external actors—for example, in an agency using a 'case-by-case' approach to support. The fact that a case-by-case approach is chosen does not mean that responsibilities are worked out only when a case arises. Rather, the responsibilities should be understood and defined in anticipation of the next case.

Figure 5.3

Key responsibilities for positive reporting climate

Table 1: Key ingredients of a positive reporting climate

Ingredient	Employee statement	Key responsibilities				
		Junior management	Middle management	Internal investigators	Senior management	Law/policy/ CMC
1 Obligation to report	'It's my job to report my concerns.'	x	x		x	X
2 Clear understanding of internal witness roles	'I can report without getting tagged as a troublemaker.'		x	x		X
3 Good internal investigation systems	'I can trust the agency to investigate this quickly, fairly and accurately.'		x	X	x	x
4 Internal witness support strategies	'My managers will take steps to see I don't suffer unnecessarily.'	x	X	x	x	x
5 Responsiveness to reprisals	'If anyone undertook a reprisal, they'd be in trouble.'		x	X		x
6 Recognition	'The agency will thank me in the end.'		X		x	

X indicates where primary responsibility for this issue lies at the present time.

x indicates where key additional/supplementary responsibilities lie.

Source: Brown et al. (2004).

Figure 5.4 provides a further example of the roles and responsibilities of key players in a 'standing program'. Organisations can use this table to identify key officers who are responsible for ensuring all staff who report wrongdoing are supported and protected.

Figure 5.4

Roles and responsibilities of key players

	Senior managers	Managers and supervisors	Specialist area	All staff
Leading by example to create an organisational culture that encourages, values and supports disclosing	✓	✓		
Ensuring that strategies to prevent public interest wrongdoing are included in the organisational business plan so that they are treated as an integral part of work activities	✓			
Ensuring that procedures for making, receiving and managing PIDs are in place and evaluated on a regular basis	✓		✓	
Ensuring employees have access to information on your organisation's policy and reporting options	✓	✓		
Receiving PIDs made orally or in writing	✓	✓	✓	
Forwarding all PIDs and supporting evidence to your organisation's specialist area	✓	✓		
Supporting disclosers	✓	✓	✓	✓
Linking the discloser to other support mechanisms	✓	✓	✓	
Identifying and addressing any risks of reprisal that the discloser may face	✓	✓	✓	
Ensuring that PIDs are addressed quickly and effectively	✓	✓	✓	
Taking all reasonable steps to ensure that disclosers are not subject to reprisals or any form of detrimental action	✓	✓	✓	
Ensuring that the rights of those who are the subject of a PID are protected and natural justice is accorded	✓		✓	
Keeping confidential the identity of the discloser and subject(s) of the PID	✓	✓	✓	✓
Deciding on what appropriate action to take following a PID	✓	✓	✓	
Ensuring that all involved in conducting investigations understand the principles of the WP Act	✓		✓	
Taking action following the outcome of any investigation or review, including taking any disciplinary or management action required	✓	✓	✓	
Implementing organisational change necessary as a result of a PID	✓	✓	✓	
Reporting offences to the appropriate authorities, particularly criminal offences to the police and official misconduct to the CMC	✓		✓	
Establishing clear lines of authority and accountability	✓	✓		
Implementing staff awareness and training		✓	✓	
Disclosing public interest wrongdoing	✓	✓		✓
Identifying areas where opportunities for public interest wrongdoing may occur and/or management systems are inadequate	✓	✓	✓	✓
Reporting on the number of PIDs received each year and their outcomes	✓		✓	

Source: Crime and Misconduct Commission et al. (2009).

Roberts | Brown | Olsen

SEPARATION OF INVESTIGATION AND SUPPORT FUNCTIONS

The common experience of the case-study agencies, especially those with standing support programs, is that the organisational approach to whistleblowing should recognise the incompatibility of the same individuals trying to investigate disclosures or alleged detrimental action in relation to a whistleblower, and seeking to provide them with support.

Some evidence of the rationale for this principle is found in the first report and noted in Section D1 dealing with sources of internal witness support. It was notable that 'internal investigation' units ranked as a significant source of whistleblower support, but that their value tended to decrease when things became difficult (Brown and Olsen 2008a:215). This result follows the logical reality that, in many instances, while investigators might be highly sympathetic and a source of crucial advice to whistleblowers, they might not be able to substantiate the allegation or arrive at a conclusion that the whistleblower supports. Further, their responsibility is to move on to the next investigation or other duty, rather than provide ongoing support.

REPORTING LINES OF SUPPORT PERSONNEL

Figures 5.1 and 5.2 emphasise the importance of support personnel having clear and direct lines of reporting to whichever organisational levels are necessary to influence management decisions relevant to a whistleblower's welfare. This might include the need to recommend that certain action be stopped or initiated.

This 'access to the top' is likely to be particularly important in devolved or case-by-case programs, where practical support lies more heavily on a designated confidant or mentor with less central institutional support. In this case, the duty of such a confidant to sound the alarm regarding reprisal risks or detriment by the agency needs to extend to an obligation to get involved in management decisions for which they have no normal responsibility.

Similarly, this 'access to the top' outside normal reporting lines could be very important where normal organisational policies need to be bypassed or subverted in order to secure timely action conducive to a whistleblower's welfare, such as a desired transfer, additional leave, relocation or other action.

PRACTICAL ACTION

Agencies are encouraged to determine which whistleblowing support program, and scale of program, is commensurate with their needs depending on their case load. The key lesson from the first report—discussed in Section D1—is the desirability of organisations designing a proactive support program that is management initiated, based on a comprehensive system for tracking reports at all levels of the organisation so that all employees who report or provide information in relation to wrongdoing are quickly identified, and an assessment is made as to their need for support.

It is recommended that agencies both estimate the size of the at-risk population they wish to support and make a clear choice as to which model they are going to develop to provide that support, to allow appropriate costing and staffing decisions.

The sample procedures provide guidance on describing the roles and responsibilities of different individuals involved in an organisation's whistleblowing arrangements. Not surprisingly, this is highly contextual and depends on factors such as the organisation's governance framework and size.

The separation of investigative and support functions is easiest to achieve in a standing program, where a permanent internal witness support unit can work with, but be kept institutionally separate from, an internal investigation unit.

Ensuring separation of functions becomes more complex where resources limit the location of whistleblower coordination staff to the same unit that performs other organisational integrity functions, or require a 'case-by-case' model. In these circumstances, the same principle needs to be observed to the maximum extent possible in an alternative form.

Public sector organisations are urged to ensure that their policies and procedures provide for direct lines of reporting between support personnel and a level of senior management that can influence future action. Similarly, support personnel need to have free authority to contact external agencies to ensure effective oversight of the organisation's handling of a case, where this might be required.

E2. SHARED RESPONSIBILITY FOR WHISTLEBLOWER SUPPORT

Checklist items

- Clear lines of communication to ensure manager(s) retain responsibility for their workplace and workers to the maximum extent possible.
- Clear lines of communication with external agencies regarding the incidence, nature and status of active cases.

These items reinforce the conclusions in Section D that responsibility for employee welfare—while not being left entirely to an employee's normal line-management chain—should not be removed from the duties of an employee's normal supervisors, unless circumstances positively require other arrangements.

As part of the necessary sharing of responsibility, however, the evidence regarding the frequent inability of agencies to resolve reprisal allegations means that external integrity agencies also need to be systematically included in the information flow. Where necessary, this includes decisions regarding the management of whistleblowing cases.

PRACTICAL ACTION

Organisations are encouraged to document a clear process for who is responsible for communicating with external agencies, internal centralised units, management, other support persons and the whistleblower, and when and how frequently this communication should occur. Building on the previous section, Figure 5.5 outlines some of the shared responsibilities involved in a typical case, drawing on the case-management flow diagrams of a number of agencies.

FIGURE 5.5

Shared case management

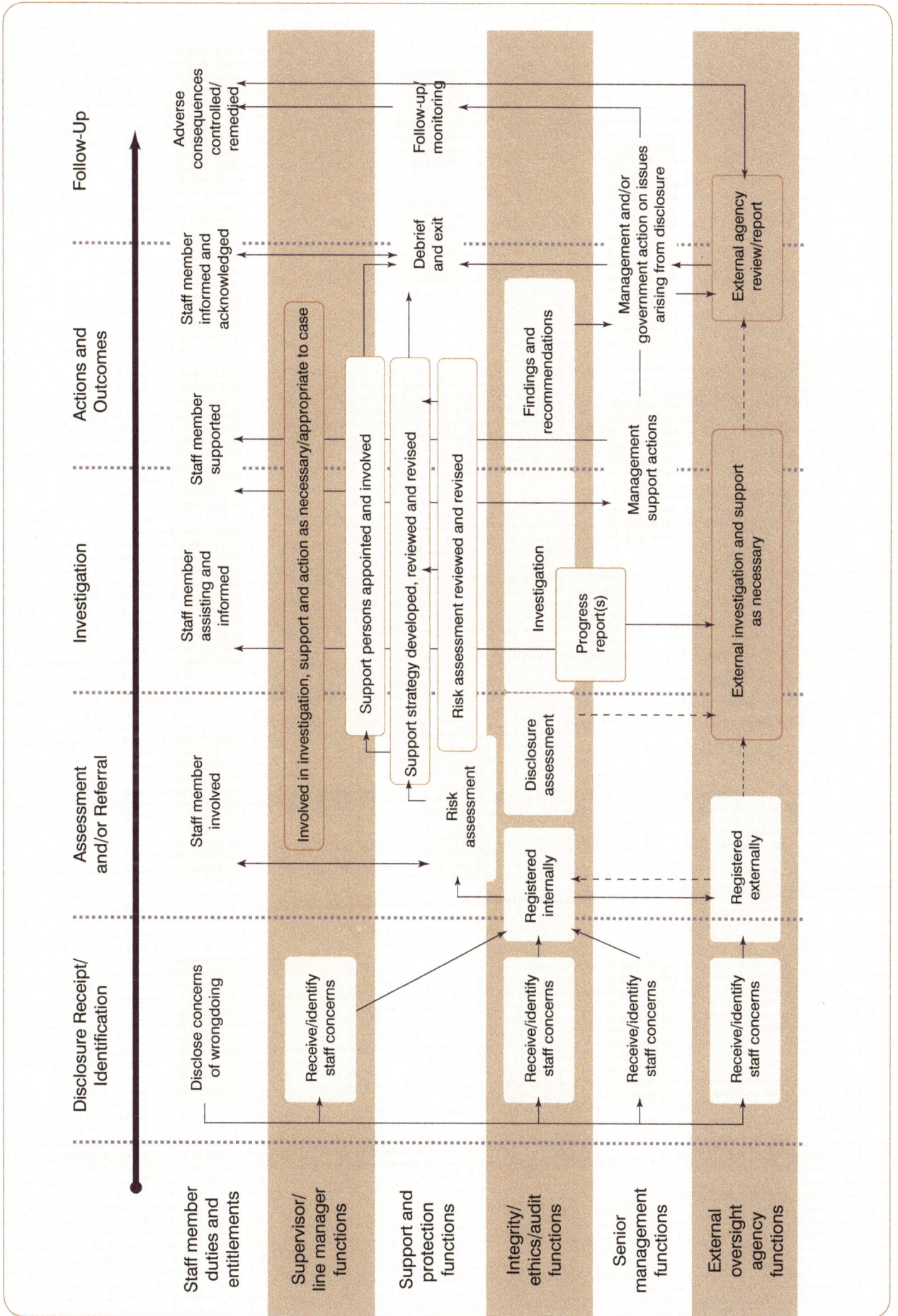

E3. EMBEDDED POLICIES AND PROCEDURES

Checklist items

- Integrated and coordinated procedures (not 'layered' or 'alternative').
- Integrated complaint/incident recording and management systems.
- Whistleblower support integrated into human resources, career development, and workplace health and safety (WH&S) policies.

These items reinforce the elements in Section A2 regarding organisational procedures, Section C1 regarding integrated disclosure tracking and assessment systems, and Sections D1 and D3 regarding the integration of whistleblower support into other policies dealing with organisational wellbeing and employee welfare.

Section A2 noted the tendency for organisations to develop their whistleblowing program and its associated policy and procedures as a new 'add on' or layer placed over the top of existing procedures. Often these procedures are developed at different times (for example, first procedures on the code of conduct, others on external agency reporting requirements, then another for fraud and criminal investigations, then others for other investigations).

Unless an integrated approach is taken, there remains a risk that whistleblowing policies will simply be ignored—for example, through the use of alternative procedures to investigate wrongdoing rather than triggering the protection requirements central to whistleblowing responsibilities. A number of agencies cited the use of alternative 'tags' and investigation paths for disclosures, including their informal treatment, as alternatives to acknowledging them as public interest disclosures under whistleblowing legislation.

A similar risk attaches to the multiple types of wrongdoing into which a whistleblowing disclosure could be rightly or wrongly classified or divided, causing it to go unregistered on agency systems or to fall off the radar.

PRACTICAL ACTION

Public sector organisations are encouraged to develop a simple, consolidated set of procedures relating to organisational accountability, integrity and case handling that integrates whistleblowing roles and responsibilities with those related to the code of conduct, investigation of matters or referral to external agencies.

Finally, it is suggested that organisations demonstrate to managers that their response to reporters and whistleblowing is linked to their responsibility as public employers to provide their staff with safe, healthy workplaces, free of wrongdoing and of detrimental action, in the interests of a professional public sector, a climate of continuing high job satisfaction and equality of employment opportunity for employees who speak up about possible wrongdoing.

SAMPLE POLICIES AND PROCEDURES

Roles and responsibilities

Roles and responsibilities of the executive and senior management.

The members of the executive and senior management of the organisation are responsible and accountable for

- leading by example to create an organisational culture that gives a clear message that making reports of wrongdoing is encouraged and valued and public interest wrongdoing is not acceptable

- ensuring that strategies to prevent public interest wrongdoing are included in the organisational business plan so that they are treated as an integral part of work activities

- identifying areas where opportunities for public interest wrongdoing might occur and/or management systems are inadequate

- ensuring that procedures for making, receiving and managing reports of wrongdoing are in place and evaluated on a regular basis

- ensuring all employees have access to information on the relevant legislation and reporting channels (both internal and external) for public interest wrongdoing

- ensuring that all employees and contractors involved in managing reports of wrongdoing understand the principles of the relevant legislation, in particular confidentiality

- ensuring that internal disclosures are addressed quickly and effectively

- taking all reasonable steps to ensure that employees who make reports of wrongdoing are not subject to reprisals or any form of detrimental action

- ensuring that the rights of those who are the subject of a report of wrongdoing are protected and natural justice is accorded

- taking action following the outcome of any investigation or review, including taking any disciplinary or management action required

- implementing any organisational change necessary as a result of a disclosure

- reporting offences to the appropriate authorities, particularly that any criminal offence should be reported to the police

- supporting staff who make reports of wrongdoing

- referring to relevant internal procedures for reporting, ensuring employees have access to information on the relevant legislation, and reporting channels in the organisation.

Roles and responsibilities of managers, supervisors and team leaders.

Managers, supervisors and team leaders are responsible and accountable for

- leading by example to contribute to an organisational culture that gives a clear message that making reports of wrongdoing is encouraged and valued and public interest wrongdoing is not acceptable

- receiving reports of wrongdoing made in person or in writing (whether the reporter identifies themselves or is anonymous)

- supporting staff who make reports of wrongdoing and linking them to other support mechanisms

- identifying and addressing any risks of reprisal that the discloser might face

- ensuring that employees who make reports of wrongdoing are not subject to reprisals or any form of detrimental action

- keeping confidential the identity of the reporter and any officer against whom the report was made

- establishing clear lines of authority and accountability

- ensuring all employees have access to information on the relevant legislation and reporting channels (both internal and external) for public interest wrongdoing

- implementing staff awareness and training

- identifying areas where opportunities for public interest wrongdoing might occur and/or management systems are inadequate.

Roles and responsibilities of staff members.

All staff members are responsible and accountable for

- reporting matters where there is evidence that shows or tends to show public interest wrongdoing

- ensuring the success of the relevant legislation within their workplace

- identifying areas where opportunities for public interest wrongdoing might occur and/or management systems are inadequate

- supporting those who have made reports of wrongdoing

- keeping confidential the identity of the reporter and any officer against whom the report was made.

Roberts | Brown | Olsen

APPENDIX 1

The project involved five Australian universities and 14 partner organisations, including the public integrity and management agencies listed in the Acknowledgments and on the project web site (<http://www.griffith.edu.au/law/whistleblowing>).

ABOUT THE PROJECT

The Australian Research Council-funded Linkage Project 'Whistling While They Work: Enhancing the Theory and Practice of Internal Witness Management in Public Sector Organisations', led by Griffith University (2005–09), has examined public officers' experience of and attitudes towards whistleblowing across a wide cross-section of public agencies from the Commonwealth, NSW, Queensland and WA Governments.

The project involved four other Australian universities and 14 partner organisations, including the public integrity and management agencies listed in the Acknowledgments and on the project web site (<http://www.griffith.edu.au/law/whistleblowing>). A steering committee representing the partner organisations oversaw the project, while the project team consisted of the lead researchers from each participating university plus three partner investigators, from the NSW, Queensland and WA public sectors.

The research aim was to identify and expand 'current best-practice' systems for the management of public interest disclosures in the Australian public sector, including more effective whistleblower protection. By undertaking empirical research into the performance and potential of existing internal witness management approaches, the project sought to develop new standards for internal disclosure procedures in public sector integrity systems, foster improved coordination between integrity bodies in the handling and oversight of disclosures, and support implementation of improved internal witness management strategies in a range of organisational settings.

The four main objectives of the research have been

- to describe and assess the effects of whistleblower legislative reforms on the Australian public sector over the past decade, including effects on workplace education, willingness to report and reprisal deterrence

- to study comparatively what is working well and what is not in public sector internal witness management, to inform best-practice models for the development of formal internal disclosure procedures and workplace-based strategies for whistleblower management

- to identify opportunities for better integration of internal witness responsibilities into values-based governance at organisational levels, including improved coordination between the roles of internal and external agencies, and strategies for embedding internal witness responsibilities in good management

- to inform implementation strategies for best-practice procedures in case-study agencies, including cost-efficient options for institutionalising and servicing such procedures in a range of organisational, cultural and geographic settings, as well as legislative and regulatory reform where needed.

THE SURVEYS

As set out in the first report (Brown 2008:15–21), eight surveys were employed in the project to collect data on individual experiences and institutional practices.

- The **Agency Survey** provided data on the extent, content and operation of whistleblowing procedures in agencies (n = 304).

- Similar data on practices and procedures were sought from specialist integrity agencies in each jurisdiction—including partner organisations to the project—through a corresponding **Integrity Agency Survey** (n = 16).

- The **Procedures Assessment** analysed the 175 sets of whistleblowing procedures supplied in response to the Agency Survey by comparing their comprehensiveness and completeness using a 24-item rating scale.

- The **Employee Survey** was a confidential, anonymous survey of a random sample of staff from each of the 118 participating agencies (n = 7663).

- Of these 118 agencies, 87 volunteered to participate in further research, with 15 of these agencies being selected as **case-study agencies** by the research team (see below for further information on the features and selection of the case-study agencies).

- The **Internal Witness Survey** elicited more extensive information from 242 whistleblowers across the case-study agencies.

- The **Case-Handler and Manager Survey** elicited more extensive, comparable information from these two groups within the case-study agencies (n = 828). Case-handlers (n = 315) were defined as including: internal investigation staff, audit and ethics staff; human resource management staff; internal and external (for example, contracted) employee welfare and assistance staff; and union staff.

- The **Integrity Case-Handler Survey** was distributed to relevant case-handling staff (n = 82) from specialist integrity agencies in each jurisdiction (including partner organisations).

THE INTERVIEWS

Respondents to the Internal Witness, Case-Handler and Manager Surveys were asked whether they would be willing to be interviewed on their experiences in relation to whistleblowing, and those who volunteered were subsequently contacted for an interview. In total, 92 interviews were conducted between 2006 and 2009 across the four participating jurisdictions.

	Cwlth	NSW	Qld	WA	Total
Internal witnesses	18	21	9	10	58
Case-handlers	2	4	2	4	12
Managers	1	7	9	5	22
Total	**18**	**31**	**14**	**19**	**92**

The reporter interviews were semi-structured: a schedule of key themes was utilised that focused upon getting the interviewee to relate the reason why they reported wrongdoing, the sequence of events and their experiences after reporting. More structured interviews were conducted with 34 managers, investigators and whistleblower support staff.

Interviews were conducted either by telephone or face-to-face by interviewers comprising research staff associated with the project and students. All interviews were recorded and transcribed, and each participant was given the opportunity to examine the interview transcript and make clarifications or amendments. The transcripts were coded using NVivo.

In examining the transcripts of the interviews provided by the reporters, the author was sensitive to the fact that the data being analysed were the perceptions of the reporter as to what had occurred. While managers and investigators from the case-study agencies were also interviewed, they were asked to provide general observations on their organisation's whistleblowing policies and procedures, and were not questioned about specific cases. Consequently, the detailed, fine-grained information on specific cases came only from reporters themselves and is thus interpreted accordingly.

The interviews with reporters were designed to elicit factual material in the context that the participants had come forward to relate their experiences to the project team. In line with the framework suggested by Gubrium and Holstein (2004), a constructionist approach was utilised in analysing the interview data. The transcripts were analysed to record specific factual issues as well as examining the narrative reporters were relating in presenting their version of the issue. This approach enhanced the data analysis by bringing forward key factual information while remaining cognisant of the ethnographic and phenomenological nature of the reporters' narratives.

FEATURES OF THE CASE STUDY AGENCIES

The purpose of inviting agencies to participate as case-study agencies was to examine a number of agencies' internal witness management systems in greater detail, and engage those agencies in the development of new benchmarks for best practice, both for their own use and for the benefit of agencies more generally.

A total of 87 agencies volunteered to participate in further research as case-study agencies, with 16 agencies selected by the research team for this role in May 2006. Four agencies were chosen from the Commonwealth and Queensland Governments, five agencies from New South Wales, and three from Western Australia.

The selection was based on criteria including

• size

• type/portfolio area

• approximate level of integrity risks

• presence or non-presence of relevant procedures, training and resources

• internal investigation activity and witness case load

• known or suspected good/bad practice in internal witness management.

The aim of the research team was to ensure that the case-study agencies were selected to reflect the considerable diversity among public sector agencies, and even within particular types of organisations, in terms of their nature, size and perceived risk of wrongdoing.

The majority of the case-study agencies are departments of state (n = 9), however, there are also three local governments, as well as two statutory bodies, a tertiary education body, and a government-owned corporation. The departments spanned a wide range of portfolio areas, including health, education, law enforcement and transport.

There is also great variation between the case-study agencies in terms of size, with the number of full-time equivalent employees ranging from 174 employees in the smallest agency to 110 000 employees in the largest. The most common organisational size for case-study agencies was between 1000 and 5000 employees, with seven agencies of this size.

The 16 case-study agencies were thus a representative snapshot of the larger group of 118 agencies from which the Employee Survey data set is drawn. In all, 2116 responses to the Employee Survey were received from the case-study agencies, meaning that while these agencies represent only 13 per cent of the larger group, their respondents account for 28 per cent of the total Employee Survey data set.

A further analysis of the interview data collected by the project was undertaken in the course of a doctoral project associated with the *Whistling While They Work* project (Annakin, 2011). That study focused upon whistleblowers who reported to external accountability agencies as well as their own organisations.

COMPARATIVE ANALYSIS OF THE CASE-STUDY AGENCIES

As part of the research, the case-study agencies were compared on a range of measures. One was the comprehensiveness of their written procedures (Roberts 2008).

In addition, the agencies were compared on eight key indicators relevant to whistleblowing based on the responses to the Employee Survey. The indicators used were

1 (positive) employee attitudes to reporting

2 level of employee awareness of reporting-related legislation

3 level of employee awareness of relevant policies

4 whistleblowing propensity of employees

5 trust in organisational response to whistleblowing

6 (low) inaction rate in response to perceived serious wrongdoing

7 reporters' knowledge of whether investigation has occurred

8 (positive) treatment of reporters by management following report.

These indicators were selected as a result of the analysis in the first Whistling While They Work report, from which they emerged as key, relatively objective measures of success in relation to the management of whistleblowing.

There were significant variations between agencies on many of these measures, just as the first report recorded major variations in results between agencies across the board. The guide contain charts comparing the case-study agencies—identified by the letters A through to P—against some of the criteria listed above. (Agency J participated in the Agency Survey, Analysis of Procedures, the Employee Survey and the Manager and Case-Handler Survey but not the Internal Witness Survey. Consequently, this agency appears in some of the comparative analyses, but not in others.)

The performance of agencies was then consolidated into a ranking of their overall level of success against these indicators. Individual agencies were ranked as follows.

Rank	1	2	3	4	5	6	7	8	9	10	11	12	13	14	15
Agency	B	A	M	P	N	E	C	F	D	O	L	G	K	H	I

The results were shared between representatives of the agencies in a project workshop, for the purposes of provoking discussion about their strategies for encouraging reporting and supporting whistleblowers. The results of this discussion, along with the quantitative data and results from interviews, were used to inform the content of this guide. Additionally, on the basis of a ranking, the authors were able to make observations about what was the most effective way of handling whistleblowers and these observations informed the suggestions in this guide.

APPENDIX 2

There are significant advantages in undertaking risk assessment at the organisational-unit level where the employee is located.

Roberts | Brown | Olsen

UNDERTAKING A RISK ASSESSMENT TO DETERMINE RISK OF REPRISALS, CONFLICTS AND ADVERSE CONSEQUENCES

WHO SHOULD UNDERTAKE THE RISK ASSESSMENT?

There are significant advantages in undertaking the assessment at the organisational-unit level where the employee is located. The advantages of this are as follows.

- It can be done quickly without having to go through the processes of being referred to a central unit. If there is some risk of reprisal then this can be recognised and acted upon early.

- Much of the information that will be used to undertake the risk assessment will emanate from line management or the employee. It would be counterproductive to refer matters to a central unit that then has to go back to the line management to find out significant information relevant to the assessment. This would take more time and make the process unnecessarily complex.

- By going through the process of assessment at the line-management level, it would remind line managers of their responsibilities to support and protect reporters, as well as provide some degree of assurance to employees under threat that their interests are being taken seriously.

There are, however, some disadvantages in undertaking the risk assessment at the line-management level. These include

- given that the research findings indicate that the most likely source of reprisals is management itself, it might be a leap of faith to assume that line managers are always going to deal with the risk assessment in a fair and reasonable manner

- risk-assessment processes, by their very nature, require some degree of skill and formality that might not be present at the local-management level

- there is a close nexus between good performance management and the effective handling of employees who come forward with reports. If the report has been triggered by shortcomings in the performance-management process then the direct line manager is clearly not a neutral source of risk-assessment advice.

Whether the risk process is conducted centrally, at the unit level, or some combination of both, it is essential that the reporter be involved in the risk-assessment process.

USEFULNESS OF RISK CHECKLIST

The research included detailed analysis of the factors that are more likely to be present when whistleblowing cases result in adverse consequences for the reporter, compared with when they do not (Brown and Olsen 2008b). These factors are a valuable pointer when thinking about risks of bad treatment (for example, reprisals) to reporters. Note that the risks for reprisals by management and co-workers differ.

Those statistical analyses, however, only indicate factors that correlate with less than optimal outcomes. These correlations should not automatically be interpreted as direct causation. If organisations are to fully utilise risk-management techniques to assist reporters, over time they will build up a bank of agency experience that will enable them to more accurately predict the risks of reprisals. In other words, the factors mentioned are a starting point for thinking about risk rather than being definitive.

In undertaking an initial risk assessment, the usual approach, and the one suggested here, is to set down a list of factors that can be quickly scanned and serve to alert line managers to the key problems, such as

- a specific threat against the internal witness has been received
- the issue reported is serious*
- there is more than one wrongdoer involved in the matter*
- the wrongdoing was directed at the internal witness*
- the internal witness has made a report about a more senior officer*
- the wrongdoing that is the subject of the report is occurring frequently*
- the size of the internal witness's immediate work unit is small*
- the internal witness is employed part-time or on a casual basis*
- a history of conflict with management and supervisors exists
- the internal witness has already disclosed his or her identity or they will become identified when the substance of the report is made known
- there is a history of reprisals in the work unit.

(* Derived from Brown and Olsen [2008b:137–64]).

Agencies that have kept records of their whistleblowing processes might be able to add to this checklist with items specific to that particular organisation.

RISK CHECKLIST AS A FILTER OR PRELIMINARY ASSESSMENT

Another issue for organisations when using a preliminary checklist of factors is to determine whether or not that initial risk assessment is going to be used as a filter, or as the first stage in a more comprehensive risk analysis to be undertaken by a central whistleblower-handling unit. These are issues specific to each organisation and decisions need to be made in the light of the existing risk-management structures and skills of managers.

APPLYING THE RISK-MANAGEMENT STANDARD

As mentioned above, virtually all public sector agencies have adopted risk-management practices as part of their everyday operation. The key documents in this process are

- International Standard ISO31000 (2009). *Risk management standard*
- Standards Australia (2004). HB436:2004 *Risk management guidelines: Companion to AS/NZS4360:2004 Risk management standard.*

The risk checklist described above is not a risk assessment in accordance with the principles of the International Standard ISO31000 (2009), but only a suggested starting point.

The practice and implementation of risk management are almost universal in the Australian public sector. Consequently, it is reasonable to assume that the technical capacity to apply the risk-management process does not need reiterating and only the part of the risk-management process that is directly relevant to reporter reprisals needs to be dealt with here.

DETERMINING APPROPRIATE RISK CRITERIA

A key element that would differentiate whistleblowing from the application of risk management to other topics is the selection of appropriate risk criteria. (There is often

Roberts | Brown | Olsen

some confusion about the notion of risk criteria. Put very simply, it is the dimension of consequence that can be scaled so as to enable some form of measurement of the risk. In many circumstances, risk criteria are quite obvious—for example, when analysing fraud risks, the usual criteria are financial loss and damage to reputation.) In a whistleblowing context, there could be four risk criteria

- harm to the reporter
- performance/efficiency of the organisation
- resources
- reputation of the organisation.

SETTING ACCEPTABLE LEVELS OF RISK

The whole purpose of undertaking a risk assessment is to make a decision as to what needs to be done. Logic dictates that there will be a level of risk set above which action is taken and below which no action is taken. While this is an issue for each organisation to determine, acceptable risk levels against each criterion could be the following.

- **Harm to the reporter.** Both good management practice and obligations to have a safe workplace would lead to the conclusion that there would be a low threshold of acceptable risk when it comes to harm to people within the organisation. The risk level should comprehend immediate and long-term impacts.

- **Performance/efficiency of the organisation.** With this criterion, organisations do have some room to manoeuvre.

- **Resources.** Similar to the above, most public sector organisations would have some discretion in this regard. A very large public sector organisation, however, would have much greater resources at its disposal to deal with one particular case than a much smaller organisation such as a local government authority.

- **Reputation of the organisation.** Very few organisations welcome adverse media attention and it is generally accepted that the threshold here would be reasonably low.

Ideally, in setting acceptable risk levels, the description of the level should be set in such precise terms that anyone in the organisation is clear as to what is the actual level of acceptable risk

Once this step has been concluded, the remaining steps of the standard should be applied.

REFERENCES

Roberts | Brown | Olsen

Annakin, L. (2011). *In the public interest or out of desperation? The experience of Australian whistleblowers reporting to accountability agencies (Unpublished PhD thesis)*. University of Sydney, Sydney.

Australian Government 2010, *Government Response to the House of Representatives Standing Committee on Legal and Constitutional Affairs: Whistleblower Protection: A comprehensive scheme for the Commonwealth public sector 17 March*, Commonwealth of Australia, Canberra, <http://www.aph.gov.au/house/committee/laca/whistleblowing/report/GovernmentResponse.pdf>.

Brown, A. J. 2006, 'Public interest disclosure legislation: towards the next generation', *Journal*, <http://www.griffith.edu.au/__data/assets/pdf_file/0015/151314/full-paper.pdf>.

Brown, A. J. (ed.) 2008, *Whistleblowing in the Australian Public Sector: Enhancing the theory and practice of internal witness management in public sector organisations*, ANU E Press, Canberra.

Brown, A. J., Latimer, P., McMillan, J. and Wheeler, C. 2008a, 'Best-practice whistleblowing legislation for the public sector: the key principles', in A. J. Brown (ed.), *Whistleblowing in the Australian Public Sector: Enhancing the theory and practice of internal witness management in public sector organisations*, ANU E Press, Canberra, pp. 261–88.

Brown, A. J., Magendanz, D. and Leary, C. 2004, *Speaking Up: Creating positive reporting climates in the Queensland public sector*, Crime and Misconduct Commission, Brisbane.

Brown, A. J., Mazurski, E. and Olsen, J. 2008b, 'The incidence and significance of whistleblowing', in A. J. Brown (ed.), *Whistleblowing in the Australian Public Sector: Enhancing the theory and practice of internal witness management in public sector organisations*, ANU E Press, Canberra, pp. 25–52.

Brown, A. J. and Olsen, J. 2008a, 'Internal witness support: the unmet challenge', in A. J. Brown (ed.), *Whistleblowing in the Australian Public Sector: Enhancing the theory and practice of internal witness management in public sector organisations*, ANU E Press, Canberra, pp. 203–32.

Brown, A. J. and Olsen, J. 2008b, 'Whistleblower mistreatment: identifying the risks', in A. J. Brown (ed.), *Whistleblowing in the Australian Public Sector: Enhancing the theory and practice of internal witness management in public sector organisations*, ANU E Press, Canberra, pp. 137–64.

Brown, A. J. and Wheeler, C. 2008, 'Project findings: an agenda for action', in A. J. Brown (ed.), *Whistleblowing in the Australian Public Sector: Enhancing the theory and practice of internal witness management in public sector organisations*, ANU E Press, Canberra, pp. 289–312.

Crime and Misconduct Commission 2007, *Facing the Facts (Guidelines): CMC guide for dealing with suspected official misconduct in Queensland public sector agencies*, Crime and Misconduct Commission, Brisbane, <http://www.cmc.qld.gov.au/asp/index.asp?pgid=10841>.

Crime and Misconduct Commission, Queensland Ombudsman and Public Service Commission 2009, *Public Interest Disclosure Guides for Queensland Public Sector Organisations and Officers*, Crime and Misconduct Commission, Queensland Ombudsman and Public Service Commission, Brisbane, <http://www.ombudsman.qld.gov.au/PublicationsandReports/PublicInterestDisclosures/tabid/339/Default.aspx>.

Donkin, M., Smith, R. and Brown, A. J. 2008, 'How do officials report? Internal and external whistleblowing', in A. J. Brown (ed.), *Whistleblowing in the Australian Public Sector: Enhancing the theory and practice of internal witness management in public sector organisations*, ANU E Press, Canberra pp. 883-108.

Gubrium, J. F. and Holstein, J. A. 2004, 'The active interview', in D. Silverman (ed.), *Qualitative Research: Theory, method and practice*, Second edition, Sage, London and Thousand Oaks, Calif., pp. 140–61.

House of Representatives Standing Committee on Legal and Constitutional Affairs 2008, *Roundtable Discussion 9 September 2008: Whistleblowing protections within the Australian government public sector*, Commonwealth of Australia, Canberra, <http://www.aph.gov.au/hansard/reps/commttee/r11128.pdf>.

House of Representatives Standing Committee on Legal and Constitutional Affairs 2009, *Whistleblower Protection: A comprehensive scheme for the Commonwealth public sector*, Commonwealth of Australia, Canberra.

Independent Commission Against Corruption (ICAC) 2009, *A Guide to Conducting Internal Investigations: Fact finder July 2009*, Independent Commission Against Corruption, Sydney, <http://www.icac.nsw.gov.au/preventing-corruption/responding-to-corrupt-conduct/internal-investigations/1535>.

Mazerolle, P. and Brown, A. J. 2008, 'Support for whistleblowing among managers: exploring job satisfaction and awareness of obligations', in A. J. Brown (ed.), *Whistleblowing in the Australian Public Sector: Enhancing the theory and practice of internal witness management in public sector organisations*, ANU E Press, Canberra, pp. 165–80.

Miceli, M. P. and Near, J. P. 1984, 'The relationships among beliefs, organisational position, and whistle-blowing status: a discriminant analysis', *Academy of Management Journal*, vol. 27, no. 4, pp. 687–705.

Mitchell, M. 2008, 'Investigations: improving practice and building capacity', in A. J. Brown (ed.), *Whistleblowing in the Australian Public Sector: Enhancing the theory and practice of internal witness management in public sector organisations*, ANU E Press, Canberra, pp. 181–202.

NSW Ombudsman 2009, *Protected Disclosure Guidelines*, Sixth edition, NSW Ombudsman, Sydney, <http://www.ombo.nsw.gov.au/publication/PDF/guidelines/Protected%20disclosures%20guidelines%206th%20edition.pdf>.

Robbins, S. P., Judge, T. A., Millett, B. and Waters-Marsh, T. 2008, *Organisational Behaviour*, Fifth edition, Pearson Prentice Hall, Frenchs Forest, NSW.

Roberts, P. 2008, 'Evaluating agency responses: the comprehensiveness and impact of whistleblowing procedures', in A. J. Brown (ed.), *Whistleblowing in the Australian Public Sector: Enhancing the theory and practice of internal witness management in public sector organisations*, ANU E Press, Canberra, pp. 233–60.

Smith, R. and Brown, A. J. 2008, 'The good, the bad and the ugly: whistleblowing outcomes', in A. J. Brown (ed.), *Whistleblowing in the Australian Public Sector: Enhancing the theory and practice of internal witness management in public sector organisations*, ANU E Press, Canberra, pp. 109–36.

Wortley, R., Cassematis, P. and Donkin, M. 2008, 'Who blows the whistle, who doesn't and why?', in A. J. Brown (ed.), *Whistleblowing in the Australian Public Sector: Enhancing the theory and practice of internal witness management in public sector organisations*, ANU E Press, Canberra, pp. 53–82.